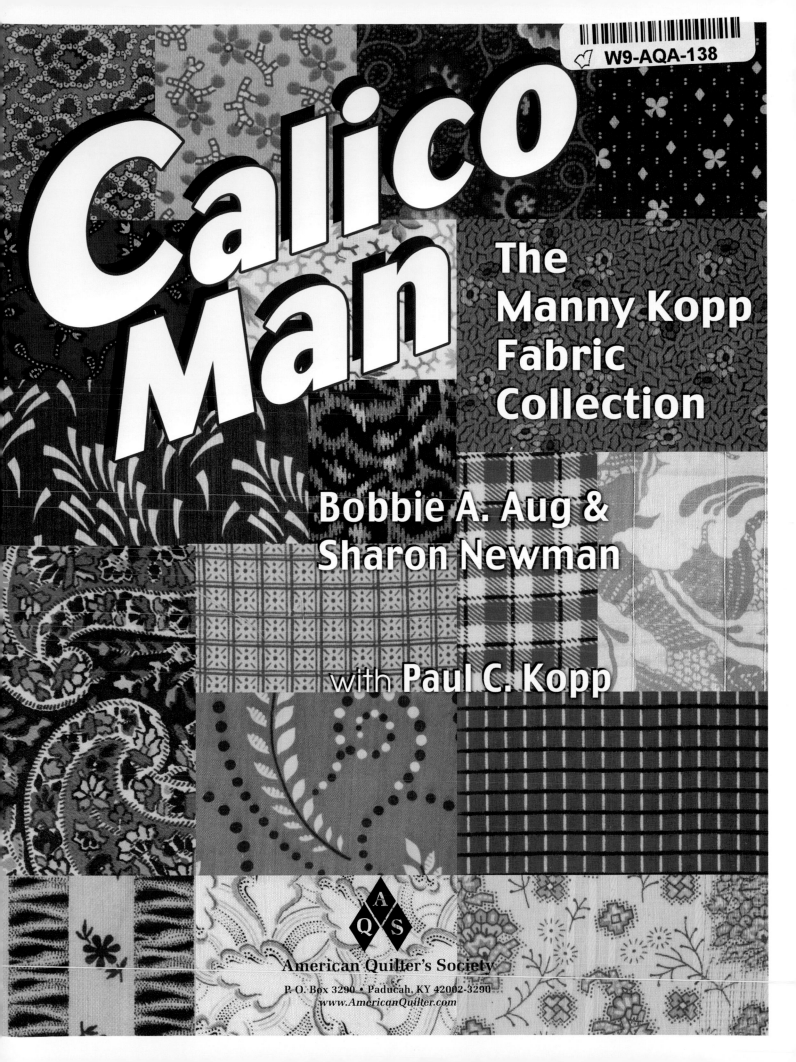

Calico Man

The Manny Kopp Fabric Collection

**Bobbie A. Aug &
Sharon Newman**

with **Paul C. Kopp**

American Quilter's Society

P. O. Box 3290 • Paducah, KY 42002-3290
www.AmericanQuilter.com

Dedication

This book is dedicated to the memory of Manny M. Kopp. It is he that we honor for leaving us his legacy to share.

Acknowledgments

The initial driving force behind this project was Paul Kopp's close friend, Louis J. Frezza. It was his enthusiasm that made this book possible.

We would like to thank Barbara D. Kopp for her continued support and encouragement, and Katie Adams for the foresight to hire Paul for that very first lecture.

In addition, we are grateful to the American Quilter's Society for believing in the Calico Man's legacy. Specifically, thanks to our editors Shelley Hawkins and Barbara Smith, associate publisher Jay Staten, and publisher Meredith Schroeder. We also appreciate the support early on in this project from Billy Schroeder, president of Schroeder Publishing.

Located in Paducah, Kentucky, the American Quilter's Society (AQS) is dedicated to promoting the accomplishments of today's quilters. Through its publications and events, AQS strives to honor today's quiltmakers and their work and to inspire future creativity and innovation in quiltmaking.

EDITOR: SHELLEY HAWKINS
GRAPHIC DESIGN: LYNDA SMITH
COVER DESIGN: MICHAEL BUCKINGHAM
PHOTOGRAPHY: CHARLES R. LYNCH

Library of Congress Cataloging-in-Publication Data
Aug, Bobbie A.
    The calico man : the Manny Kopp fabric collection / by Bobbie A. Aug and Sharon Newman.
        p.cm.
    Summary: "Assortment of nineteenth-century, early American and vintage fabrics collected by Manny Kopp from mills in America and Europe. Over a thousand fabric samples shown including calico, plaids, stripes, conversation prints, flannelettes, indigoes, leno weaves, mourning prints and others"--Provided by publisher.
    Includes bibliographical references.
    ISBN 1-57432-894-8
    1. Kopp, Manny, 1910-1991--Art collections--Catalogs.
2. Textile fabrics--Private collections--United States--Catalogs. I. Newman, Sharon, 1942-2005 II. Title.
NK8803.K67A94 2005
746'.09'034074--dc22
                2005015013

Additional copies of this book may be ordered from the American Quilter's Society, PO Box 3290, Paducah, KY 42002-3290; 800-626-5420 (orders only please); or online at www.AmericanQuilter.com. For all other inquiries, call 270-898-7903.

Contents

Preface

In the summer of 2001, we had the opportunity to hear Mr. Paul C. Kopp lecture about the extensive fabric collection that his father, Manny M. Kopp, amassed during his career as a textile designer. Since Manny's death, Paul has shared what is thought to be the largest privately owned collection of early American and vintage fabrics with interested groups and historians.

The sample fabrics that Paul brought and shared that day overwhelmed the audience. We, too, were overwhelmed. Given our quilt history background, we realized that seeing this fabric collection was a rare opportunity. People expressed disappointment that this unique collection wasn't published in a book format for study and reference. It was then that Paul approached us for assistance.

After studying this immense, cataloged fabric collection, we agreed to collaborate with Paul on a book project so that others interested in textile history could experience its significance. Most of the fabrics in this collection were grouped by style or manufacturer. Because the ledger pages were extremely fragile, we thought it was best to leave this arrangement pretty much like Manny Kopp had chosen.

It is important to note that America, England, and France all copied prints from one another. Fabrics were reproduced almost from the beginning of the mechanized printing industry. Often, the changes that were made to the reproduction fabrics were so subtle that it is very difficult to tell which piece is the original and which is the reproduction. In some cases, there were no changes. Companies would reprint the same patterns exactly as they had been decades earlier. These practices cause confusion and difficulty when determining the date of textiles. We have endeavored to be as accurate as possible in the fabric descriptions.

We are so grateful to Manny Kopp and his son, Paul, for preserving these small pieces of textile history for future generations to learn from and enjoy.

BOBBIE A. AUG
SHARON NEWMAN

Foreword

I feel fortunate to have been born to parents with so much artistic talent. My mother was a musician who shared her expertise with students. My father was a painter and artist, designing fabric and clothing for much of his life. This book is about my father, Manny M. Kopp.

Growing up, I knew that he was a perfectionist who was deeply immersed in his artwork. I didn't understand a lot of what he was doing, but could sense that he was trying to share his emotions of art and design with me. My father's love of art influenced me so much that I became an artist, and later an art teacher. He never criticized my art, which gave me room to grow.

Although we did not become close until later in life, I always knew that my father loved me and was concerned about my well-being and happiness. He supported me at each turn of my life. When I was in college, we had a Father and Son art show at Lord & Taylor in New Jersey. Sharing this experience with my father is one of my fondest memories.

I was aware early on that my father made his living in the textile business. He was the subject of many newspaper and magazine articles, such as *The Saturday Evening Post*, which reflected his importance to the trade. Until some years after his death, I had no idea that he was gathering a huge, historical textile collection and actively lecturing about its importance.

I inherited many boxes from my father's estate. My wife, Barbara, and I moved several times over the years and hauled these boxes along with us, not aware of the contents. They were nearly thrown out on more than one occasion. Barbara thought the boxes contained some cloth — perhaps old rags. I couldn't imagine old material being of much value, except that my father must have thought the contents to be important. Upon seeing a newspaper advertisement from a quilting guild looking for lecturers, Barbara called and said her husband might like to lecture. "He has some old fabrics," Barbara explained to Katie Adams, former vice president and program chair of the Coral Springs Quilters in Florida.

Katie arranged my first lecture and it finally became necessary to open the boxes. We were shocked, for what we found were my father's lecture notes, biographical information, and letters and correspondence from various organizations and groups to which he lectured. There were photocopies of canceled checks and receipts reflecting fabric sales to national institutions, and there were salesman sample books, ledgers, and paste-ups of thousands of fabric swatches.

What this industry meant to my father and how determined he was to share this history and enjoyment with others became evident. It felt like opening a treasure box to which I had the key. Maybe I could continue my father's passion of sharing this fabulous collection, while honoring his memory and contribution at the same time. I gave that first lecture September 27, 1995. Following my father's notes closely, I learned right along with the audience. By the end of the lecture, I received a standing ovation. I realized how much I, too, enjoyed sharing this historical documentation of the fabric industry. Had it not been for quilters looking to enhance their knowledge, we might have never shared this collection with you today.

In reading my father's notes and the articles written by and about him, it is abundantly clear that he loved fabric. He immersed his life totally in fabric and was renowned for his expertise in textile design. He wanted to share his appreciation for design and knowledge with other people. Because he was so dedicated to sharing the collection, I know he would be pleased to have it published. I can think of no greater way of honoring him and his legacy.

PAUL C. KOPP

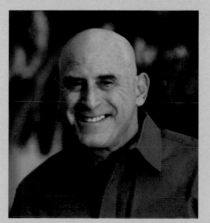

Paul and his wife, Barbara, reside in Margate, Florida, and have raised two children. Their daughter, Alissa R., also resides in Florida, and their son, David J., is a student at Clemson University in South Carolina.

Career & Legacy of the Calico Man

Manny M. Kopp was born in Berdichev, Russia, March 29, 1910, and came to the United States with his family at the age of four. He attended Brooklyn public schools and received formal art education at the Pratt Institute. He won the Pratt Wanamaker Medal for one of his paintings. In 1928, he entered the design business, realizing a lifelong dream of becoming a textile designer.

After marrying, he and his wife, Sylvia, lived in Manhattan, New York. Manny reigned in the textile design business, while Sylvia was a businesswoman in the textile industry, traveling a great deal. Some years later, they moved to Fair Lawn, New Jersey, where Sylvia was devoted to being a musician and music teacher. She gave piano lessons in their home, while raising their son, Paul. Having two artistically talented parents, it is not surprising that Paul pursued art with a passion.

Spending over 50 years in the fabric design business, Manny was a top designer for major textile companies, and owned several companies himself. During his career, he designed for Regal Textiles, Calvin Mills, Kopp and Siegel, Award Designs, Gallery Designs, Screen Fashions, Trissi Inc., and others. His expertise was born while visiting a large northeast textile mill early in his career. English and French samples of calico prints, dating to the early nineteenth century, were sold to the colonies during the early days of our country's textile industry development. Manny noticed swatches of these beautiful printed fabrics being casually tossed into trash piles on the mill floor.

What had been discarded as materials too difficult to duplicate or no longer fashionable, Manny began collecting and preserving. For nearly 40 years, he amassed a collection of thousands of American, English, and French textiles. These collected samples, ranging from ca. 1800

Manny Kopp's lecture notebook. Manny and his wife, Sylvia, are pictured here with his fabric collection.

6

to 1926, were cataloged into books while he researched their designs or origins. As Manny's collection grew, so did his reputation. He became known as a textile historian, specializing in early American fabrics, and was eventually dubbed, "The Calico Man."

Manny shared his compendium of calico textile collections by lecturing to colleges, museums, and other groups. In 1974, he began a hobby of creating early Americana fabric collages, which were gold-leaf painted designs over geometrical swatches of antique cloth framed under glass. The detail and craftsmanship shown in these designs have not been matched.

In August 1974, he was quoted in the Ridgewood, New Jersey, newspaper as stating, "Many of the materials worn today are copied from designs a hundred years old." A comprehensive exhibition of these early American fabrics and collages was presented to the public in 1976 at

the Montclair Art Museum in New Jersey, and also displayed at the American Folk Art Museum in New York City. When the Smithsonian Institution wanted fabric samples for displays, they contacted Manny, the man with the world's largest personal calico collection. The Metropolitan Museum of Art, the Cooper-Hewitt Museum, and others followed suit and purchased samples of the beautiful calicos, which remain in the permanent collections of many museums around the country today.

Manny's last position in the fashion design business ended in 1983 in New Jersey with the Moire Corporation of America, at which time he moved to Florida. After his retirement, he taught art classes and continued lecturing about his collection. Manny died in 1991 at the age of 81. He was dedicated to the selfless preservation of a collection that he just wanted to share with people – a collection that became his legacy.

Bobbie A. Aug & Sharon Newman

Introduction
Cloth in the Collection

First-Quarter Nineteenth Century

Silk continued to be imported from China, and many other fabrics such as cotton, linen, and wool were imported to America from India, England, and France. Cotton and wool were often calendared, or glazed, to create a shiny and luxurious finish. The color palette for small, stylized florals, neats, small geometrics, trailing vines, floral trails, and other tiny prints included indigo, green, pink, red, yellow, and brown. The discharge process of overprinting indigo with a chemical to release the dye and create those small figures of white discharged areas was popular.

Preprinted patchwork or "cheater cloth" designs appeared. *Toiles* that were being printed in the late 1700s continued into this period in the monotone *toiles de Jouy* color scheme of indigo, red, brown, and purple. The mechanization of the cotton printing process, and therefore the mechanized industry, began in Lowell, Massachusetts, in the early 1820s. The appreciation of finely woven cotton for linens and dress goods was apparent in the quality of fabric that was being produced in America as well as Europe.

Second-Quarter Nineteenth Century

Chintz was widely popular as a cloth of luxury. The color palette during this period included the drab combination of olive green and brown. Perhaps this combination was practical in origin because soil would not have been readily apparent.

We also found Prussian blue printed in ombré or rainbow style, bright or chrome yellow grounds with tiny overprints in black or red figures, and many greens. Besides army green, these greens included chartreuse, aqua, dark forest green, and overdyed greens with either blue or yellow streaks, depending on which color was dyed first. A deep purple could be found, especially in wool challis prints. The discharge style of printing indigo continued, and now included Turkey red as a ground. The fabrics were often then overdyed with another color, such as black, green, blue, or yellow, rather than leaving the discharged area white as previously done.

Third-Quarter Nineteenth Century

The advent of aniline or synthetic dyes brought new harsh shades not terribly unlike the early mineral dyes produced. These synthetic dyes were not necessarily any more reliable (and sometimes less) than the earlier mineral and plant dyes. The process of overdying blue and yellow to achieve green continued. With it came the same problem of the resulting green color being fugitive, leaving streaks of yellow or blue. The mass marketing of the home sewing machine created a need for increased fabric production. After the Civil War ended, there was renewed energy in the industry of cloth production and printing. New and better mordants, that resulted in new colors, and the invention of better printing technology provided new and different designs in cloth.

Shirtings were printed in many colors – not just black on a white ground. The coppery madder browns printed in stripes and reproductions of earlier paisley prints appeared following the war. Pale peach or orange, dark rich browns, and purple, which was fugitive and eventually turned to brown, could be found. Indigo remained popular because the dark color was practical, it was relatively easy to dye successfully, and it was colorfast. Double pinks and double blues printed in hundreds of differently engraved steel designs were immensely popular. We often refer to this blue as Lancaster blue. Solid Turkey red continued to be a staple. America and Europe were printing moiré patterns, eccentrics, centennial prints, and more preprinted patchwork.

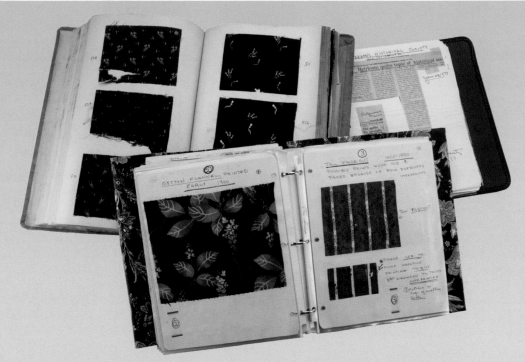

Fourth-Quarter Nineteenth Century

We often refer to this period as the Victorian period. A variety of shirting prints, "neon" prints in bright or garish yellow, green, and orange, and small dainty prints suitable for dress goods were popular. Mourning prints were gray in appearance, but might have actually been black figures printed on a white ground. These prints, as well as chocolates printed on a white ground, were dark and somber.

Conversation prints were wildly popular. On a solid ground that included indigo and red, these were printed characters, such as horseshoes, whips, tennis rackets and other sporting equipment, horses and other animals, etc. The practice of reprinting patterns that were popular in the first quarter of the century was not uncommon. Probably to meet increased need for higher production at a cheaper price, the quality of cloth declined toward the end of the century.

First-Quarter Twentieth Century

Green and purple were developed as stable dyes. Checks, plaids, and stripes abounded as the transition was made from the somewhat dark-and-dreary Victorian era to the flowery 1920s. Popular prints included chambrays in pink, blue, red, brown, navy, and green; cotton calicos in bright yellow with black or brown figures, pale pink, pale orange or peach; and reproduction calicos in larger scale. Colonial and art nouveau design, followed by art deco, influenced the printing industry. A lighter, "cadet" blue appeared in prints as well as checks, stripes, and plaids.

Quality of Cloth

Greige goods are the base fabric or muslin before any dying or printing takes place. Quality depends on the number of threads per inch in the warp and weft, as well as the thickness of the threads. During the early part of the nineteenth century, the cloth that was being produced in Europe and America was of excellent quality and aided the rapid growth of the printing industry. By the end of the century, the increased demand for cloth and the increased technology that was developed resulted in fewer colors being printed on cheaper-quality greige goods. There was also the ability to print plaids, checks, and stripes to look like woven goods, but for much less money. After World War I, the quality of fabric reverted back to good-quality greige goods for dress and home decorating.

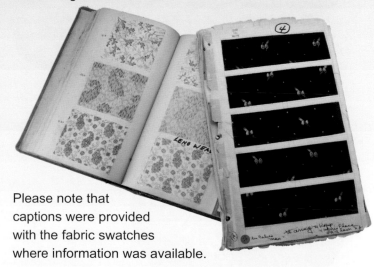

Please note that captions were provided with the fabric swatches where information was available.

FRENCH DESIGNS

These French designs are painted on paper. Eventually, the designs would have been transferred to steel mill engravings for printing on cotton. These intricate and detailed renderings could be interchanged to produce an entirely new pattern. Americans favored designs with that desirable French flair.

01–22 Original French-painted designs on paper, ca. 1874
03–08 French-painted designs, gouache and ink, 1874–1875
09–12 Red-on-white designs, 1874–1875 (page 11)
13–22 Various designs, 1874–1875 (pages 11–12)
23–32 Gouache and ink, 1874–1875 (page 12)

01

02

03

04

05

06

07

08

Calico Man – The Manny Kopp Fabric Collection

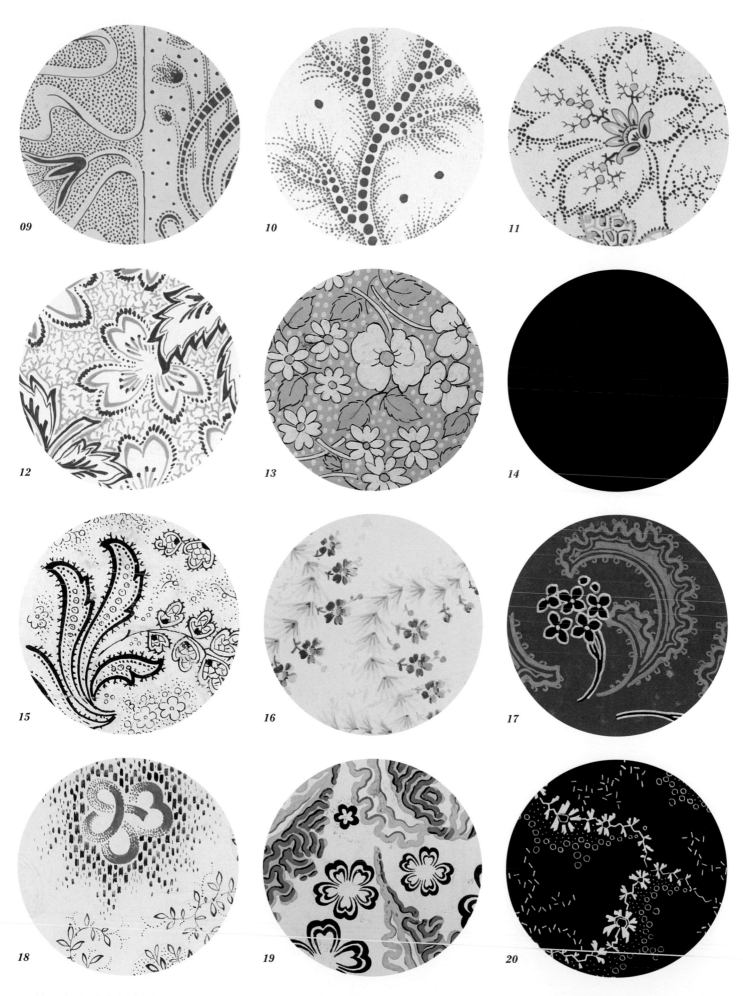

09

10

11

12

13

14

15

16

17

18

19

20

Bobbie A. Aug & Sharon Newman

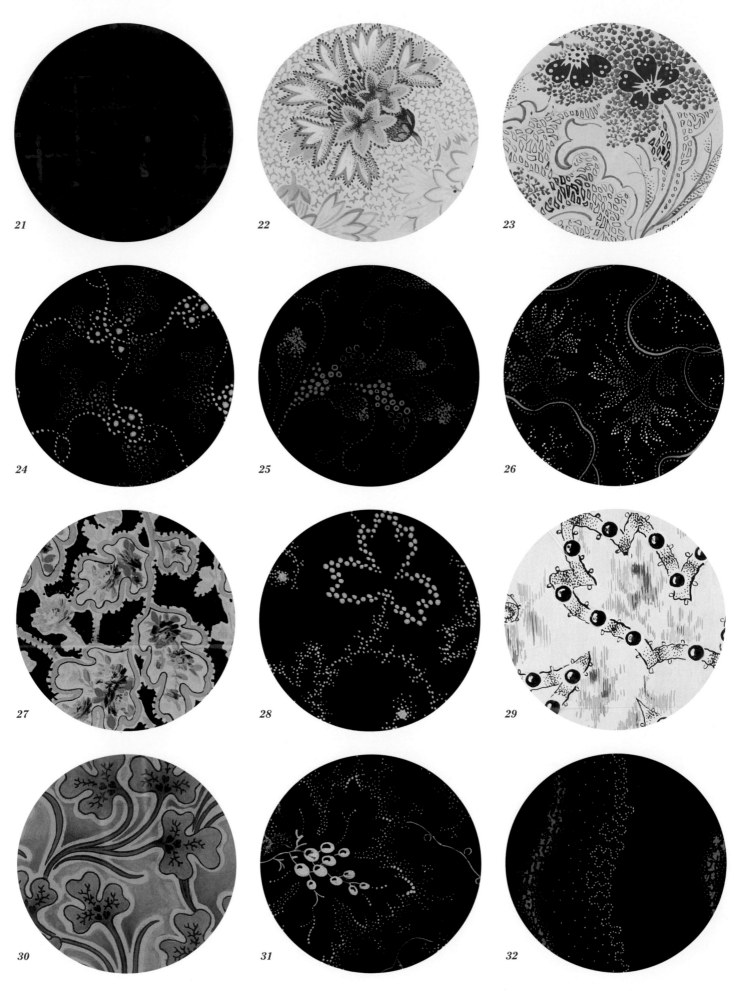

21

22

23

24

25

26

27

28

29

30

31

32

Calico Man – The Manny Kopp Fabric Collection

The Cloth

CALICO

Historically, there are many types of fiber used in the making of cloth, but cotton is thought to be the earliest. Ancient civilizations realized the importance of cotton in the production of clothing, offering protection from the elements. It was functional and later, fashionable.

We credit India with the development of fast dyes and mordants, which evolved into the commerce of printed cotton production and export to Europe by the seventeenth century. The word *calico*, which originally meant cloth made of cotton, comes from its Indian port of origin, Calicut. The meaning of calico has evolved, and it is inter-preted differently throughout the world. In Britain, for example, calico means a solid white cotton cloth, bulkier than muslin. By the 1850s in America, calico was considered to be small-scale prints, usually with a floral motif, popular in clothing as well as home décor. In this book, "calico" is defined as a cotton fabric, not strictly as a print.

Calico was inexpensive to produce – much easier and cheaper than linen production. By the 1950s, this style of print remained strong in the fabric industry. Its decline began shortly thereafter and was nearly gone from the marketplace by the end of the 1970s.

Salesman's cards sent to Poor Brothers Agents

001–002 "Lodi 630 Happy," 1902–1903 (two colorways)
003 "Lodi 629 Happen," 1902–1903
004–006 "Lodi 629 Happen," 1902–1903 (three colorways)

007–008 "Lodi 607 Gymnast," 1903 (two colorways)
009 "Lodi 608 Gyrate novelty print," 1903
010 "Lodi 607 Gymnast," 1903

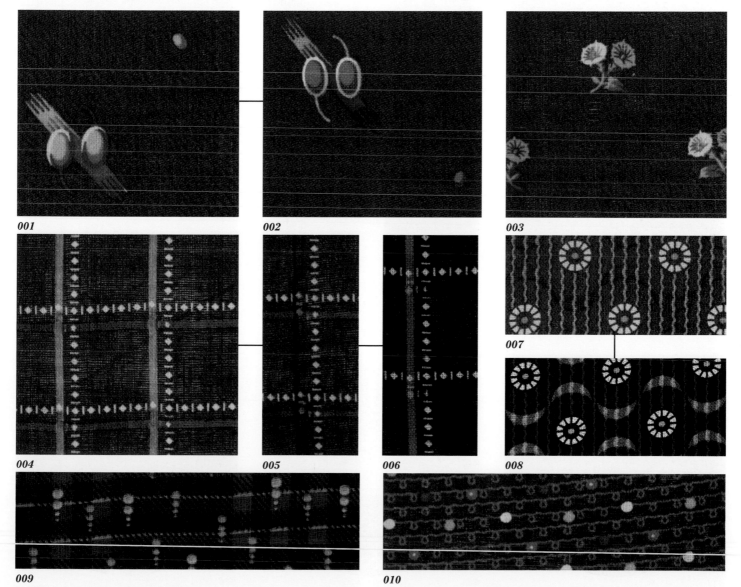

001   002   003

004   005   006   007   008

009   010

Bobbie A. Aug & Sharon Newman

CALICO

011 "Lodi 607 Gymnast," 1903

012–014 "Lodi 602 Gumbo," 1903 (three colorways)

015 "506 Apparel," 1903

016–018 "506 Apparel," 1903 (three colorways)

019–020 "506 Apparel," 1903 (two colorways)

021–023 "507 Apparel," 1903 (three colorways)

024–026 1903 (three colorways)

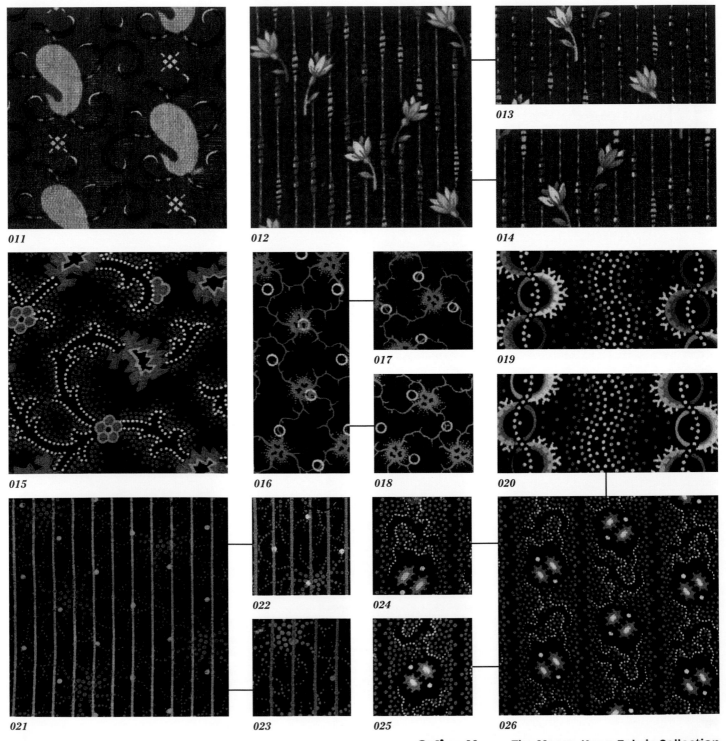

011

012

013

014

015

016

017

018

019

020

021

022

023

024

025

026

027 "506 Apparition," 1903

028–030 1903 (three colorways)

031–034 "1702 Committing," 1903 (four colorways)

035–036 "1702 Committing," 1903 (two colorways)

037 "1702 Committing," 1903

038 "1702 Committing," 1903

039 "1702 Commit," 1902

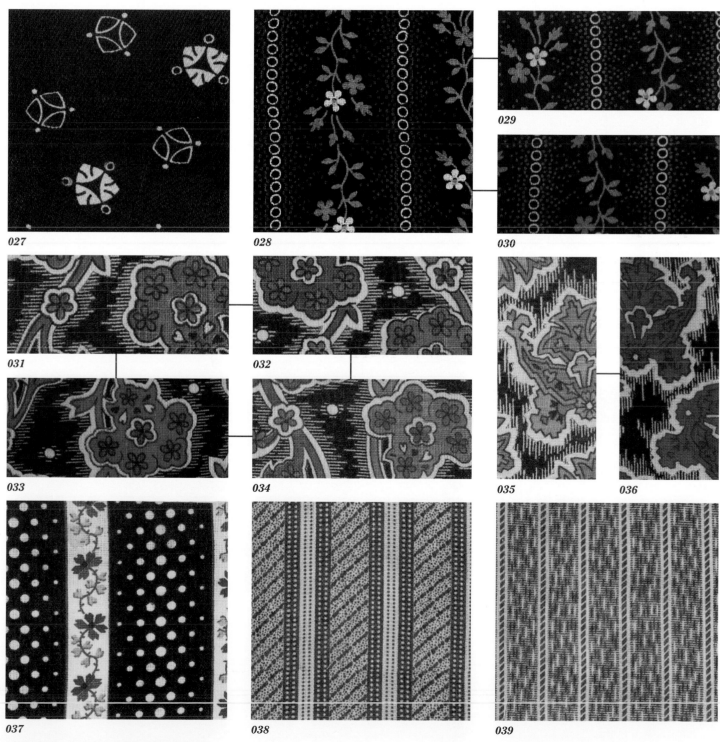

027

028

029

030

031

032

033

034

035

036

037

038

039

Bobbie A. Aug & Sharon Newman

CALICO

040–041 "1700 Committing," 1902 (two colorways)

042–044 "1701 Committed," 1902 (three colorways)

045–046 1902 (two colorways)

047–050 1902 (four colorways)

051–052 1902 (two colorways)

053–055 1902 (three colorways)

056–058 "4614 Interrupt," 1902 (three colorways)

040

041

42

43

44

045

046

047

048

051

049

050

052

053

054

055

056

057

058

059–060 "4614 Interrupt," 1902 (two colorways)
061–062 "1710 Community," 1902 (two colorways)
063–065 "1710 Community," 1902 (three colorways)

Passaic Challis Book
066–068 "Mosaic W Challis," Style 7366, 1926 (three colorways)
069–071 "Mosaic W Challis," Style 7367, 1926 (three colorways)

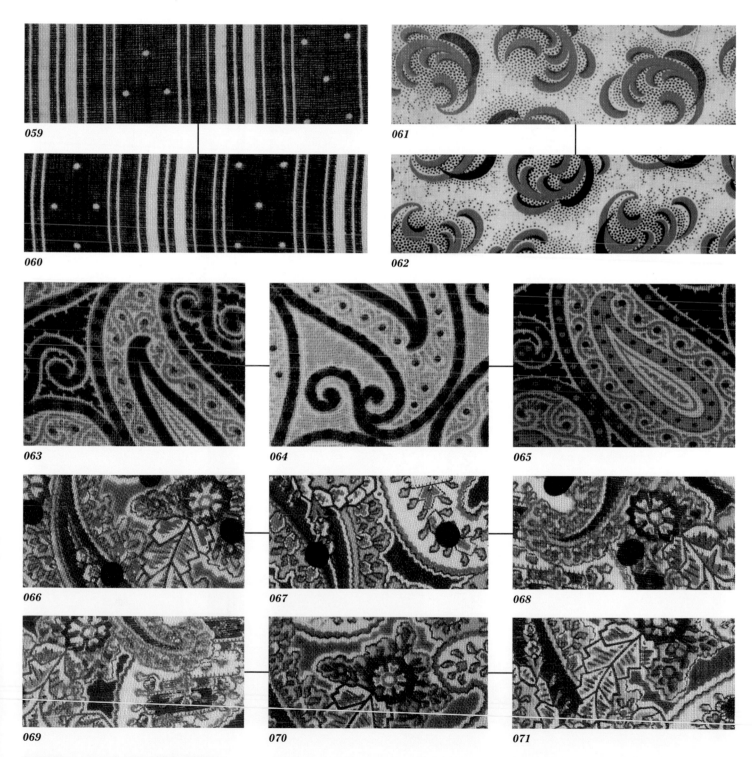

059

060

061

062

063

064

065

066

067

068

069

070

071

Bobbie A. Aug & Sharon Newman

072–074   Style 7364, 1926 (three colorways)

075–077   "Trouville Challie," Style 5028 Loaf, 1926 (three colorways)

078–081   "Trouville Challie," Style 5029 Loafing, 1926 (four colorways)

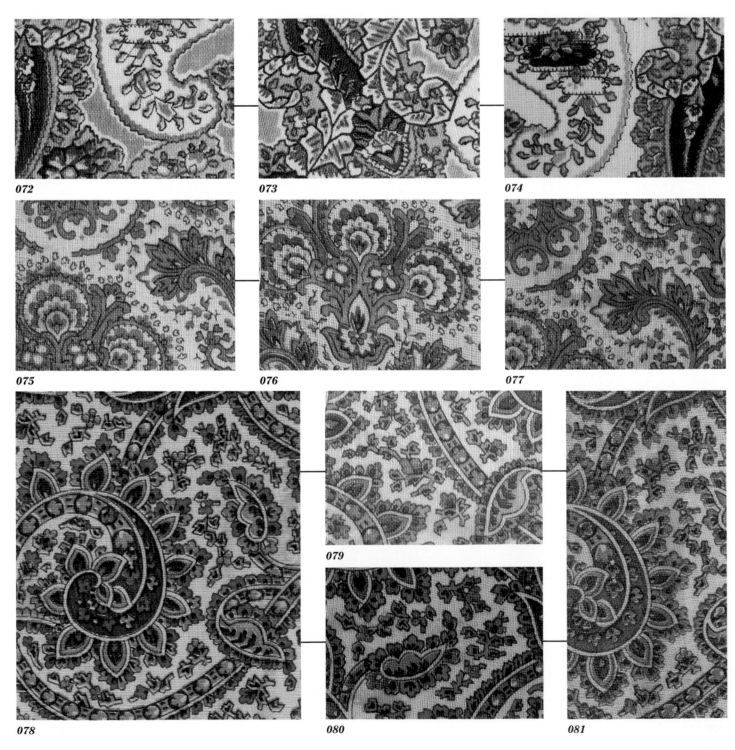

072

073

074

075

076

077

078

079

080

081

082–083 "Trouville Challie," Style 5026 Loaded, 1926 (two colorways)

084–087 "Passaic Challie," Style 7717 Curvy, 1926 (four colorways)

088–089 "Passaic Challie," Style 7718 Scuttle, 1926 (two colorways)

090–092 "Passaic W Challie," Style 7369, 1926 (three colorways)

093–096 "Passaic W Challie," Style 7368, 1926 (four colorways)

082

083

084

085

086

087

088

089

090

091

092

093

094

095

096

CALICO

097–099 "Passaic Challie," Style 7719 Scythe

100–102 "Passaic Challie," Style 7720 Seam (three colorways)

103–105 "1711 Compact," 1902 (two colorways)

106–109 "1711 Compact," 1902 (four colorways)

110–111 "1708 Communion," 1902 (two colorways)

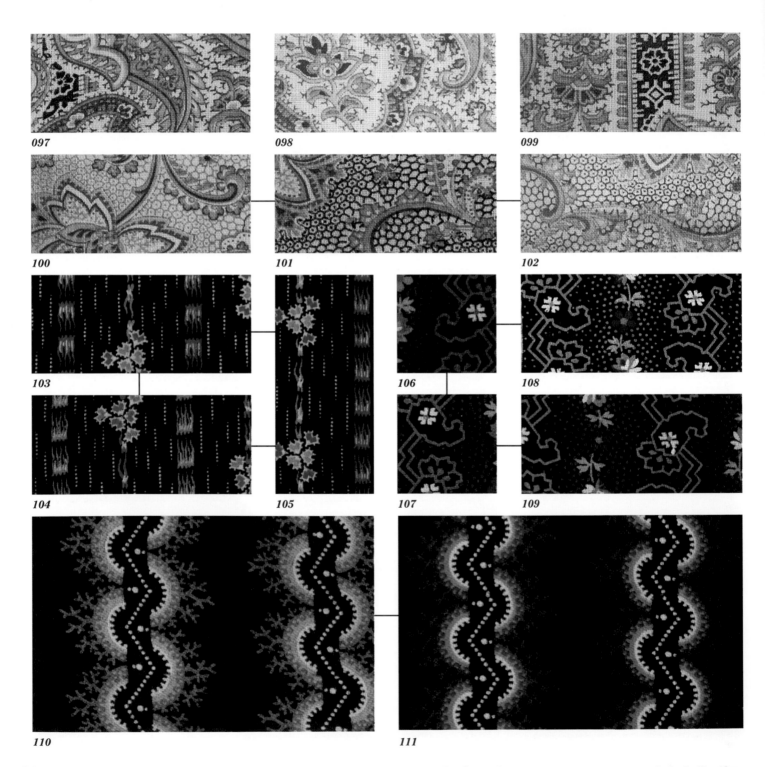

097 *098* *099*

100 *101* *102*

103 *105* *106* *108*

104 *107* *109*

110 *111*

112–114   "1708 Communion," 1902 (three colorways)

115–116   "1709 Communist," 1902 (two colorways)

117–118   1902 (two colorways)

119   "1709 Communist," 1902

120–122   "1709 Communist," 1902 (three colorways)

123   1902

124–127   "Berwick 1608 Frozen," 1902 (four colorways)

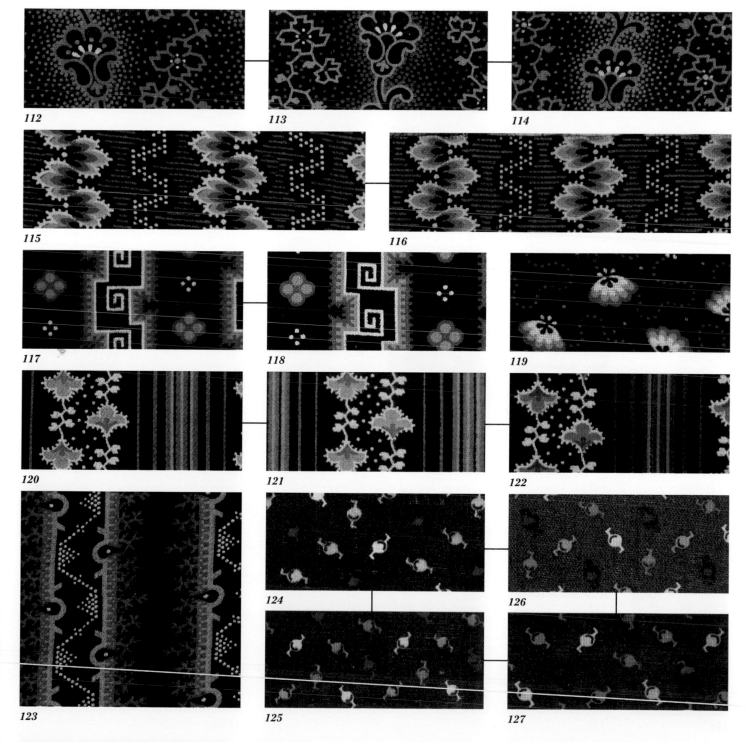

112   *113*   *114*

115   *116*

117   *118*   *119*

120   *121*   *122*

123   *124*   *126*

125   *127*

CALICO

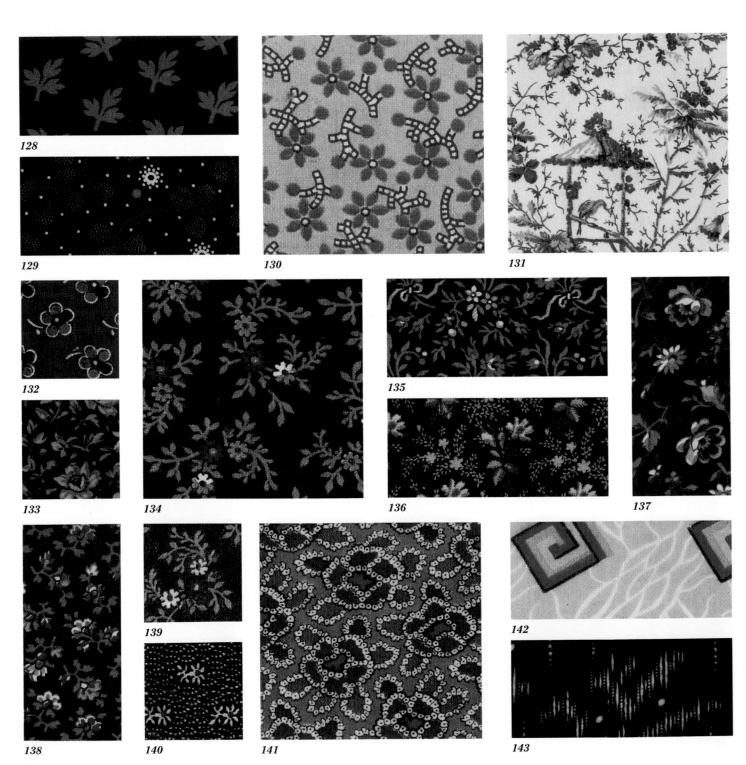

128

129

130

131

132

133

134

135

136

137

138

139

140

141

142

143

144–151 1850–1875

    152 Madder paisley, early 1850–1875

    153 Paisley print on silk, 1850–1875

144

145

146

147

148

149

150

151

152

153

CALICO

154   Fine weave, 1800–1825

155   Dye overprint, 1850–1875

156–157   1900–1925 (two colorways)

158   Late 1875–1900

154

155

156

157

158

159   1850–1875

160–163   Open sheer, 1912 (four colorways)

164   1900–1925

165   Resist large with white circles, late 1875–1900

166   Bengaline sheer floral, 1912

167–168   1875–1900

169   ca. 1900

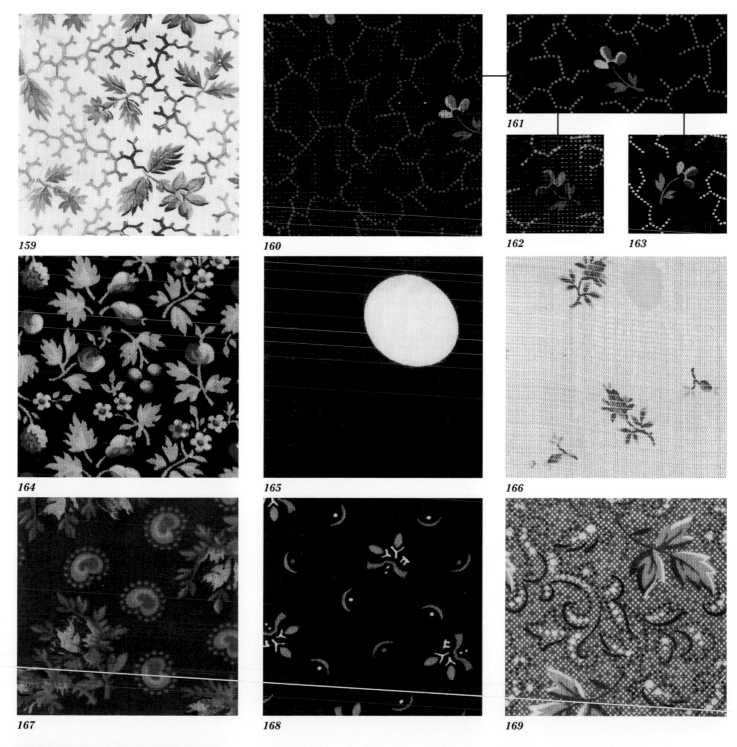

159

160

161

162

163

164

165

166

167

168

169

CALICO

170 Madder-style print, 1875–1900

171 Madder-style paisley print, 1875–1900

172 1900–1925

173 1850–1875

174 1850–1875

175 1875–1900

176–177 1900–1925 (two colorways)

178–179 1900–1925 (two colorways)

170

171

172

173

174

175

176

177

178

179

180–183 1900–1925

184 Preprinted patchwork, 1875–1900

185–186 1900–1925

187 Madder print, 1875–1900

188 Engraved ground, 1875–1900

189 1900–1925

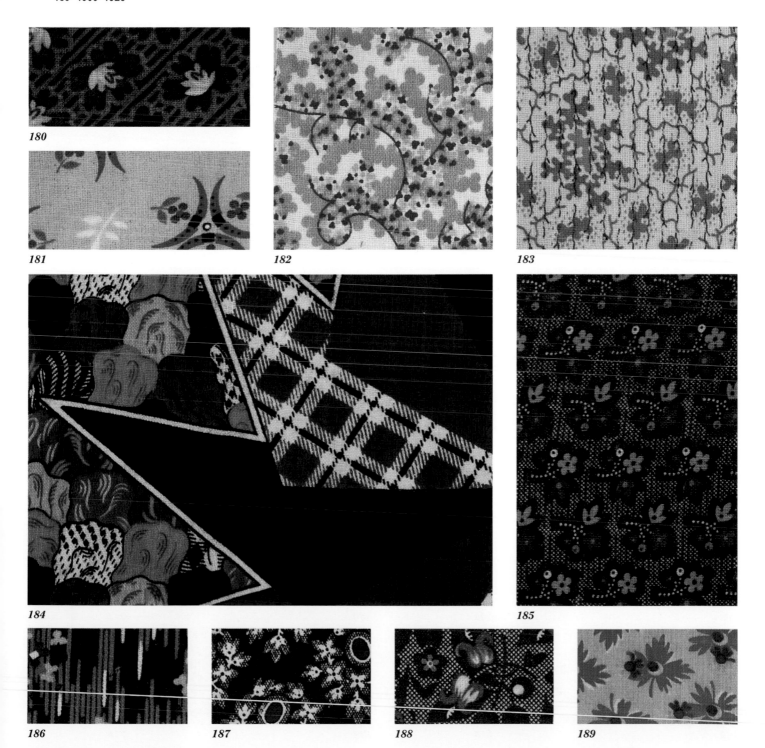

180

181

182

183

184

185

186

187

188

189

CALICO

Ledger pages

190–215 Steel engravings, 1852

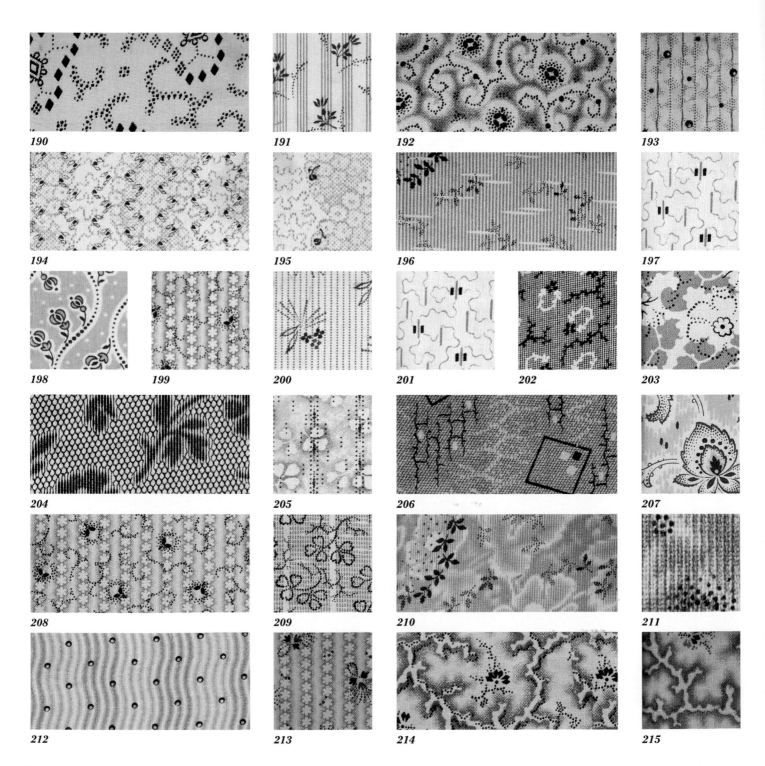

190

191

192

193

194

195

196

197

198

199

200

201

202

203

204

205

206

207

208

209

210

211

212

213

214

215

216– 217 1900–1925
218–220 1900–1925 (three colorways)
221–222 1900–1925 (two colorways)
223–224 1875–1900
225 1900–1925

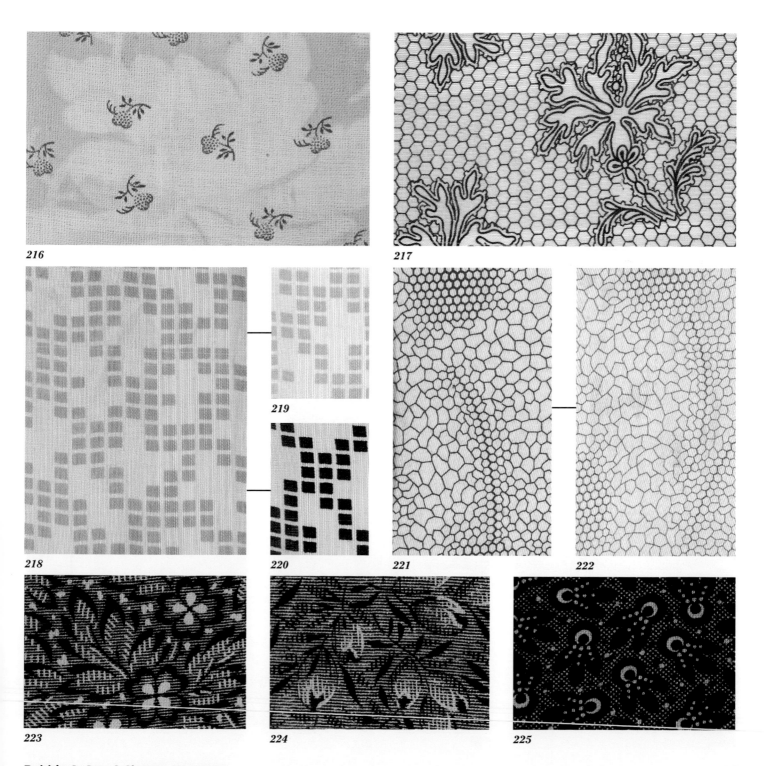

216

217

218

219

220

221

222

223

224

225

CALICO

226–235 Indigo and white, 1900–1925

226
227
228
229
230
231
232
233
234
235

236–239 1907 (four colorways)

240 1900–1925

241 Turkey print, 1875–1900

242–245 1875–1900

246–247 Turkey prints, 1875–1900

248 1850–1875

249–250 1875–1900

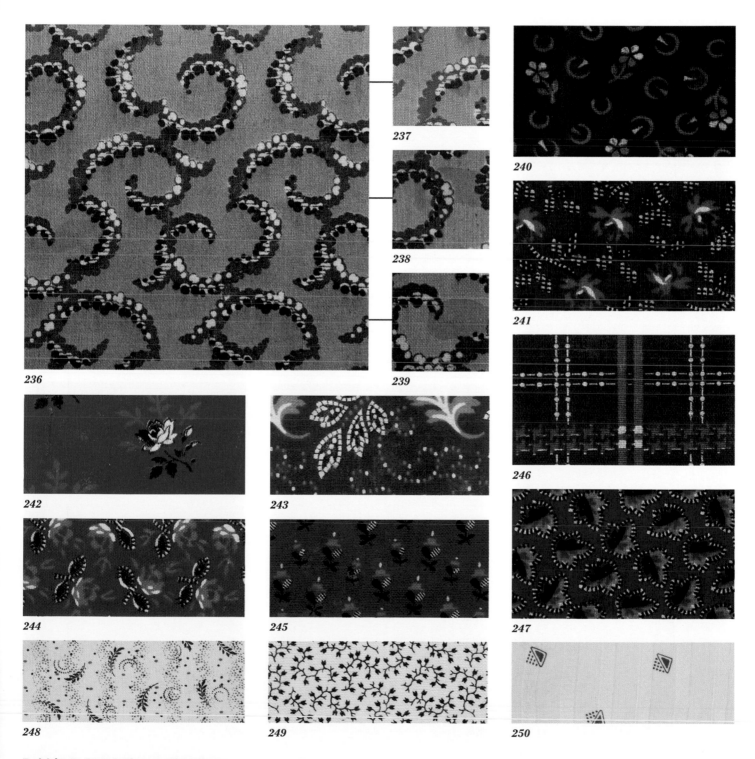

236

237

238

239

240

241

242

243

244

245

246

247

248

249

250

CALICO

251–254 Handkerchief or bandana prints (traditionally used by laborers), ca. 1900
255–257 1875–1900

251

252

253

254

255

256

257

Calico Man – The Manny Kopp Fabric Collection

258–262 Sheer French cotton floral print, 1884–1885

258

259

261

260

262

Bobbie A. Aug & Sharon Newman

263–265 Sheer French cotton paisley, 1884–1885

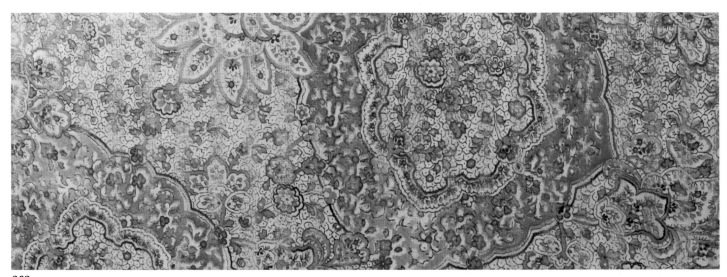

263

264

265

266–274 Finely detailed French steel mill engravings, 1852

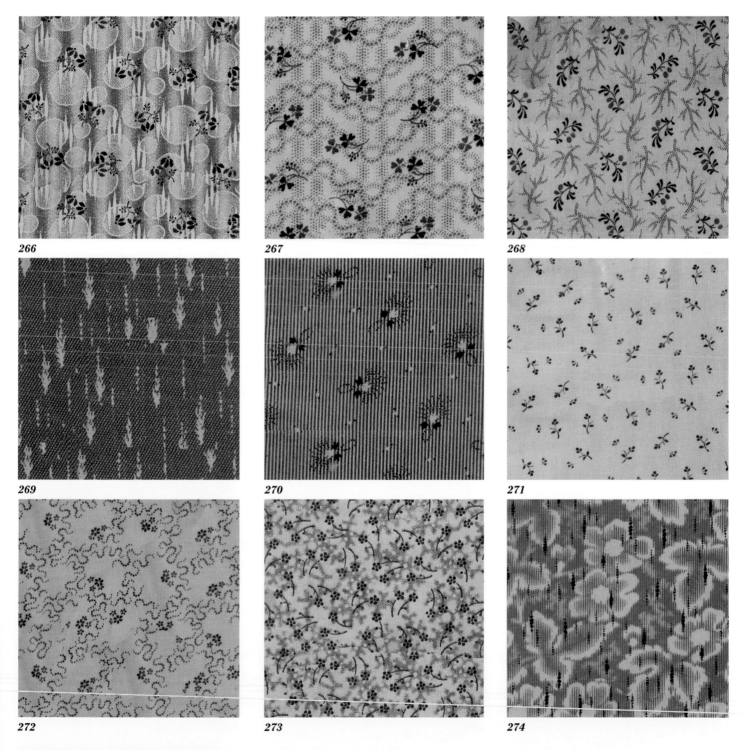

266

267

268

269

270

271

272

273

274

Bobbie A. Aug & Sharon Newman

275–283 Finely detailed French steel mill engravings, 1852

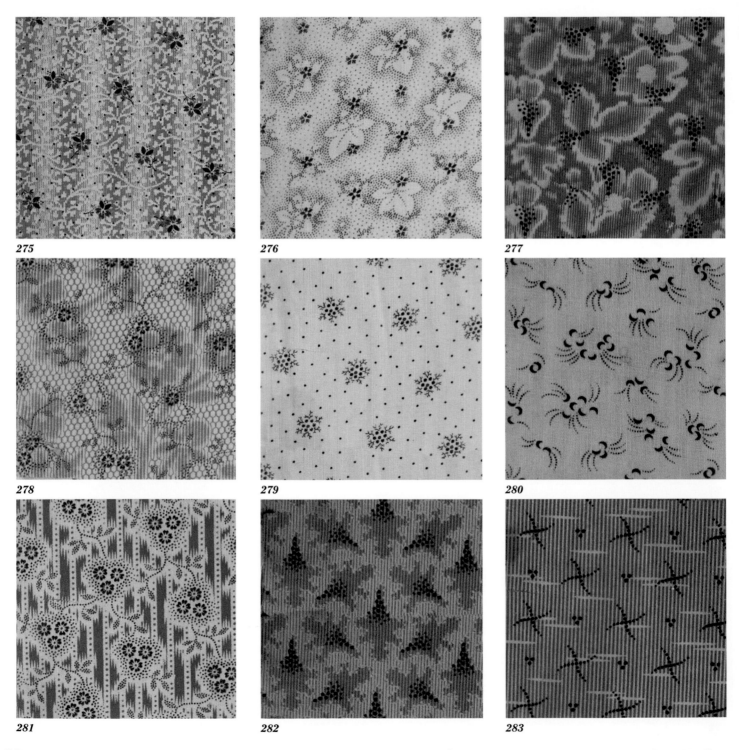

275

276

277

278

279

280

281

282

283

284–297 Finely detailed French steel mill engravings, 1852

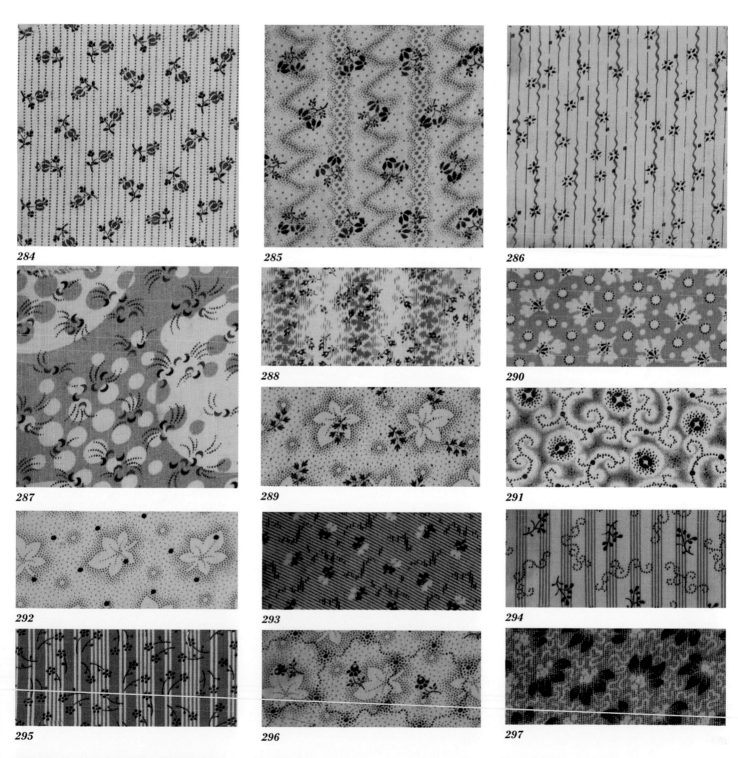

284

285

286

287

288

289

290

291

292

293

294

295

296

297

Bobbie A. Aug & Sharon Newman

298–305 Eight printer's patches from a catalog indicating the printer's notes and dye formulas (eight colorways)

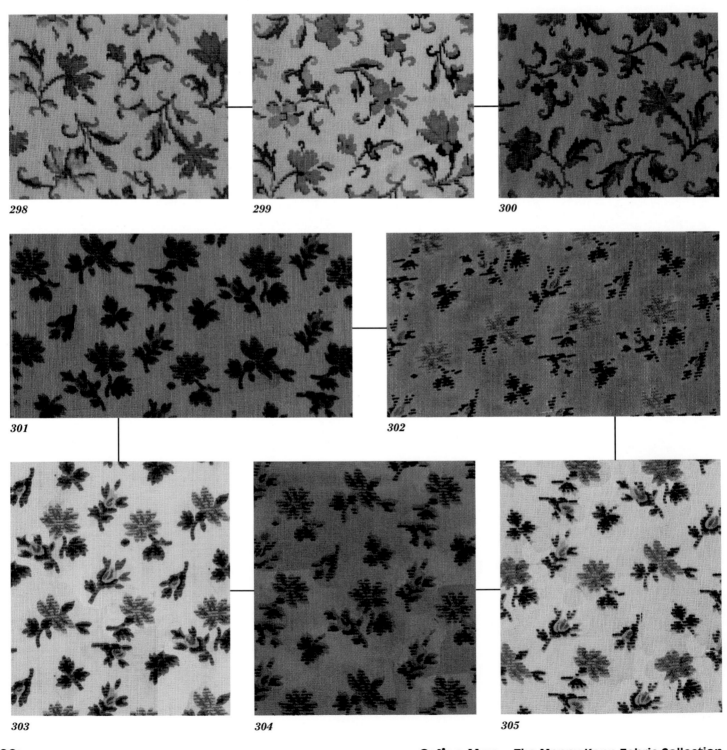

298

299

300

301

302

303

304

305

Calico Man – The Manny Kopp Fabric Collection

306–310 American prints, 1900–1925, copies of William Ashton prints from 1850–1860 (five colorways)

311–312 American prints, 1900–1925, copies of William Ashton prints from 1850–1860 (two colorways)

313 Paisley wool challis scarf, striped border print, 1900–1925

314 1900–1925

315–317 Finely engraved brown ground, 1850–1875 (three colorways)

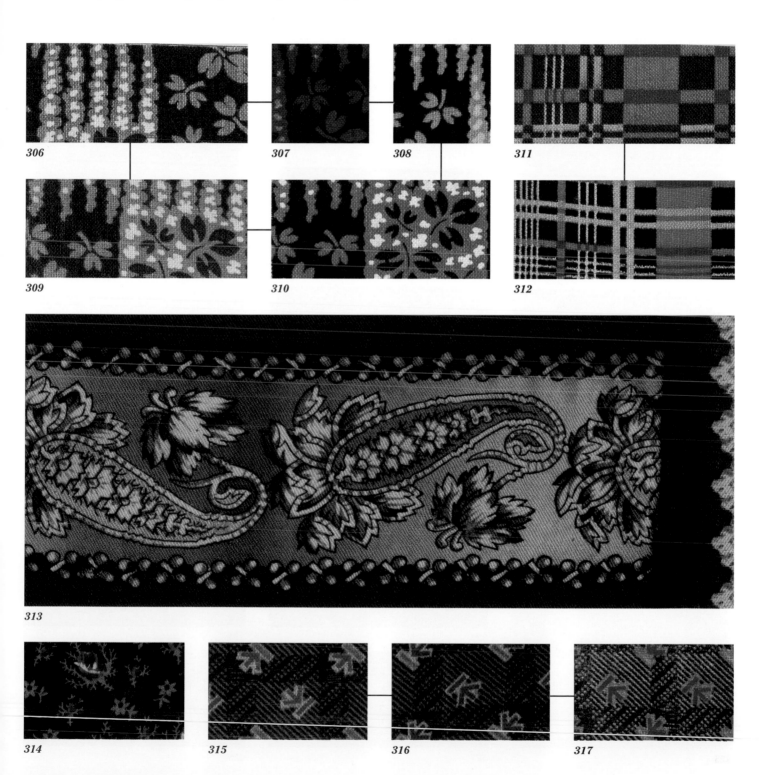

306

307

308

311

309

310

312

313

314

315

316

317

318 Blotch-printed feathers, 1850–1875

319 Blotch-printed leaves, 1850–1875

320 Blotch-printed flowers, 1850–1875

321–322 1850–1875

323 ca. 1900

324 Fine gray weave, 1875–1900

325 Fine gray weave (reproduction of an earlier print), 1875–1900

326 ca. 1900

327 1850–1875

328 1875–1900

329 ca. 1900

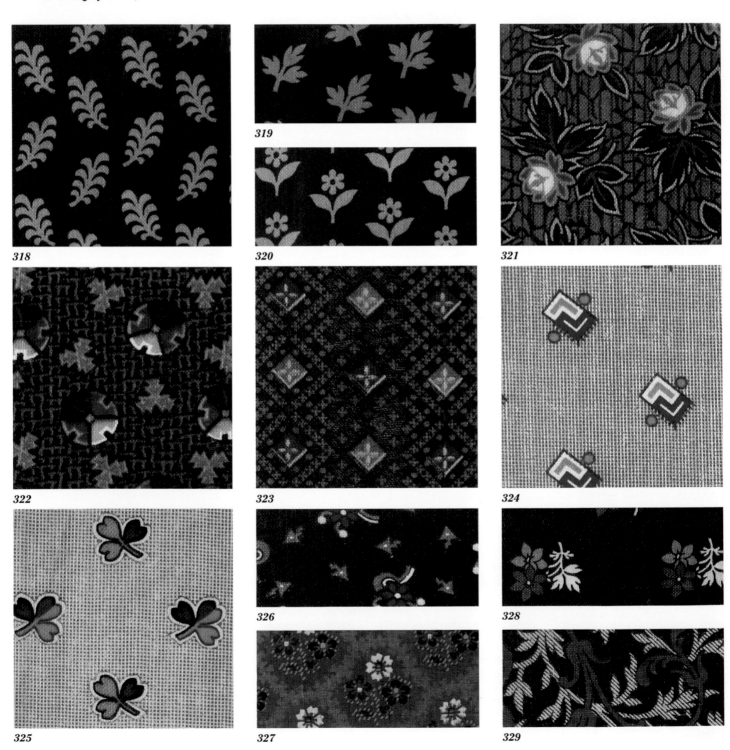

318

319

320

321

322

323

324

325

326

327

328

329

330–333 1900–1925

334–336 1900–1925 (three colorways)

337 Tapestry print, 1900–1925

338 1900–1925

339–340 1900–1925 (two colorways)

341 1900–1925

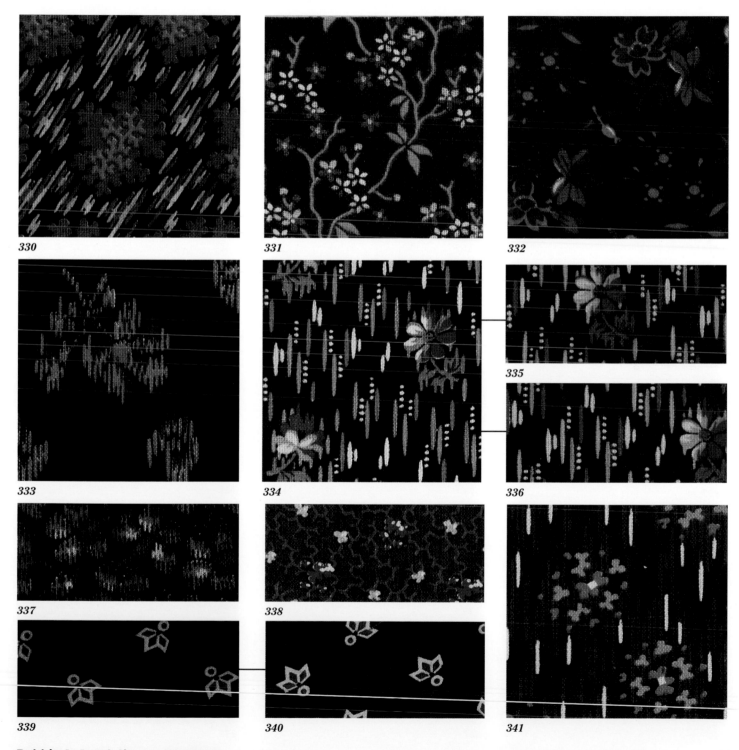

330

331

332

333

334

335

336

337

338

339

340

341

Bobbie A. Aug & Sharon Newman

CALICO

342–343 1900–1925

344 Art-deco style, ca. 1900

345–346 1900–1925 (two colorways)

347–348 Neon reproduction print, 1900–1925 (two colorways)

349 ca. 1900

350 1900–1925

351 ca. 1900

352 Neon reproduction print, 1900–1925

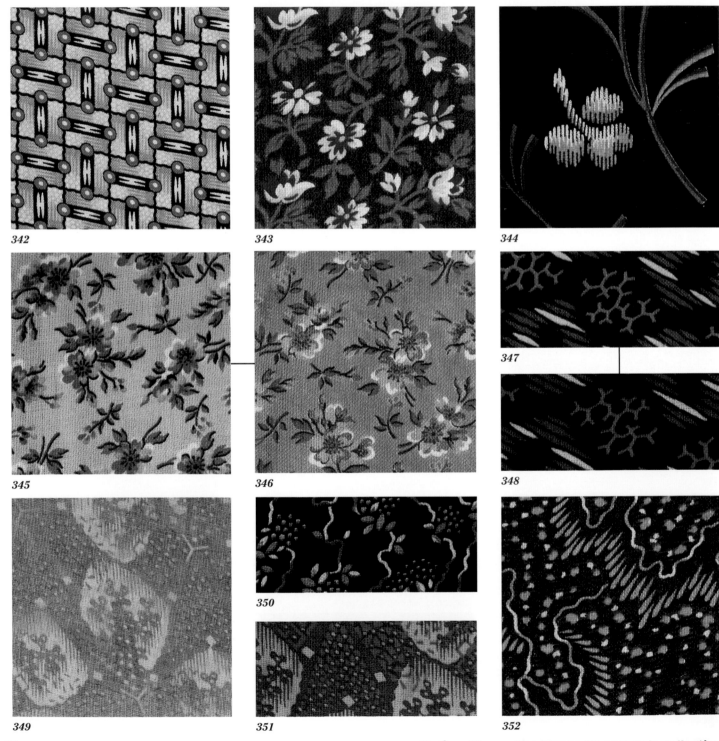

342

343

344

345

346

347

348

349

350

351

352

Calico Man – The Manny Kopp Fabric Collection

353–354 1900–1925 (two colorways)

355 1900–1925

356–357 1900–1925 (two colorways)

358–360 1900–1925 (three colorways)

361–363 ca. 1900 (three colorways)

353

354

355

356   357

358

359

360

361

362

363

Bobbie A. Aug & Sharon Newman

CALICO

364–365 ca. 1900

366 1900–1925

367–368 1900–1925 (two colorways)

369–370 1900–1925

371–372 1900–1925

364

365

366

367

368

369

370

371

372

373–374 1900–1925 (two colorways)

375 1900–1925

376–377 Moiré ground (reproduction), 1900–1925 (two colorways)

378 1900–1925

379–380 1900–1925 (two colorways)

381 1900–1925

373

374

375

376

377

378

379

380

381

Bobbie A. Aug & Sharon Newman

CALICO

382 Moiré ground (reproduction), 1900–1925
383 1900–1925
384 Twill ground, 1875–1900

385–387 1900–1925 (three colorways)
388 Spiderweb print, ca. 1900
389–390 1900–1925

382

383

384

385

386

387

388

389

390

Calico Man – The Manny Kopp Fabric Collection

391–392 1900–1925 (two colorways)
393–394 1900–1925
396 ca. 1900

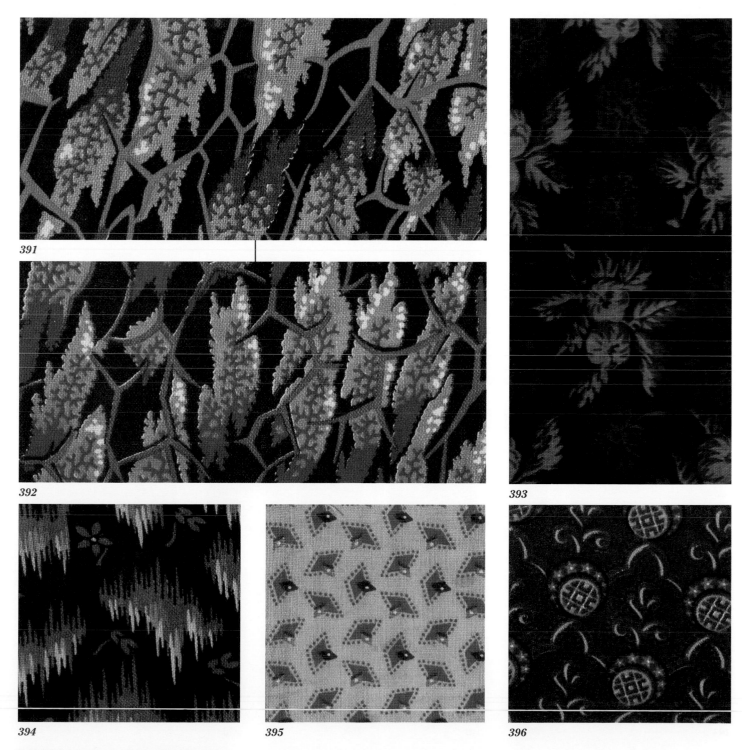

391

392

393

394

395

396

Bobbie A. Aug & Sharon Newman

"Printer's Patches and Dye Formulas" pages
397–409 ca. 1850

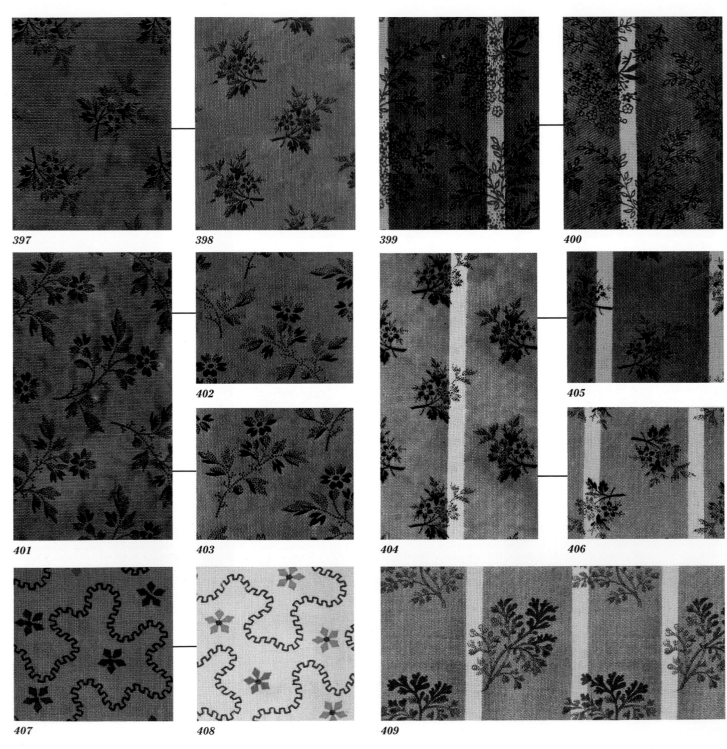

397

398

399

400

401

402

403

404

405

406

407

408

409

410–421 1875–1900

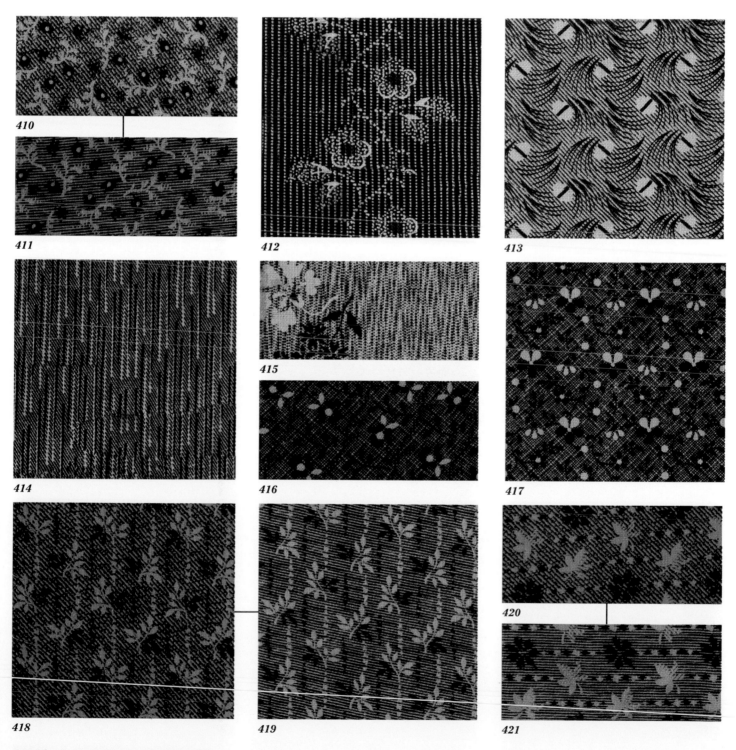

410

411

412

413

414

415

416

417

418

419

420

421

Bobbie A. Aug & Sharon Newman

CALICO

422–430 1875–1900

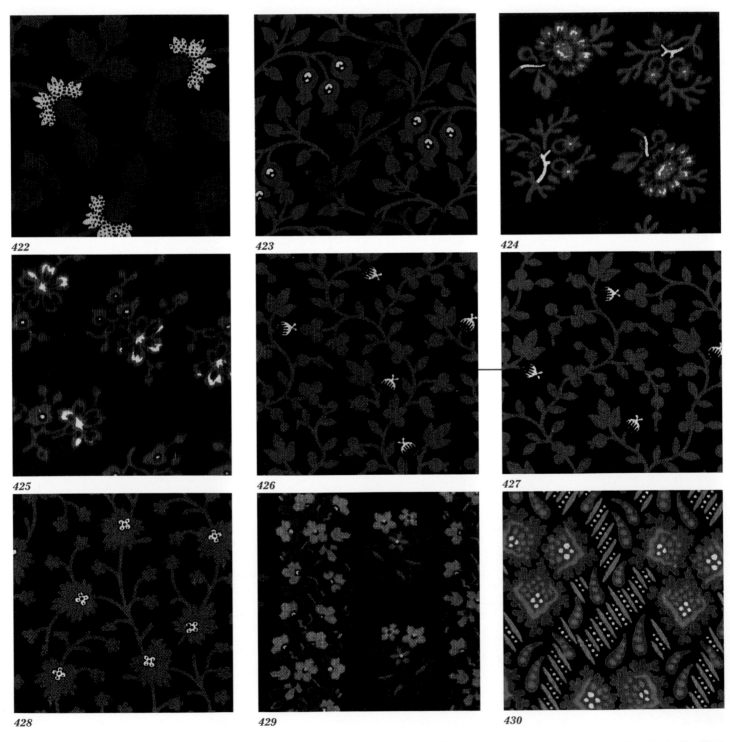

422

423

424

425

426

427

428

429

430

431– 438 1875–1900

431

432

433

434

435

436

437

438

Bobbie A. Aug & Sharon Newman

CALICO

439–448 1875–1900

439

440

441

442

443

444

445

446

447

448

449–454 1875–1900
455–456 1875–1900 (two colorways)

449

450

451

452

453

454

455

456

Bobbie A. Aug & Sharon Newman

CALICO

457–463 1875–1900

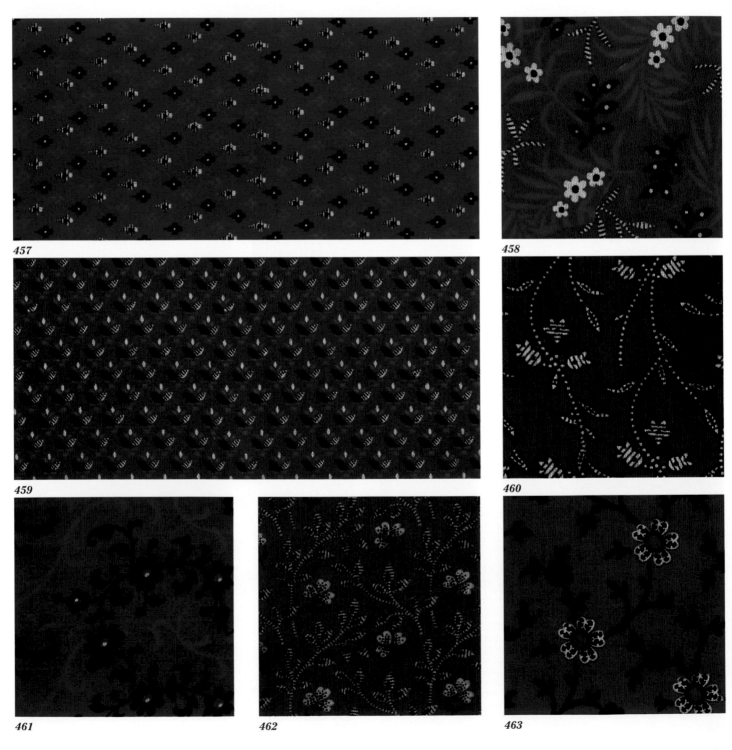

457

458

459

460

461

462

463

Calico Man – The Manny Kopp Fabric Collection

464–468 1900–1925 (five colorways)
469–473 1900–1925 (five colorways)
474–477 1900–1925 (four colorways)

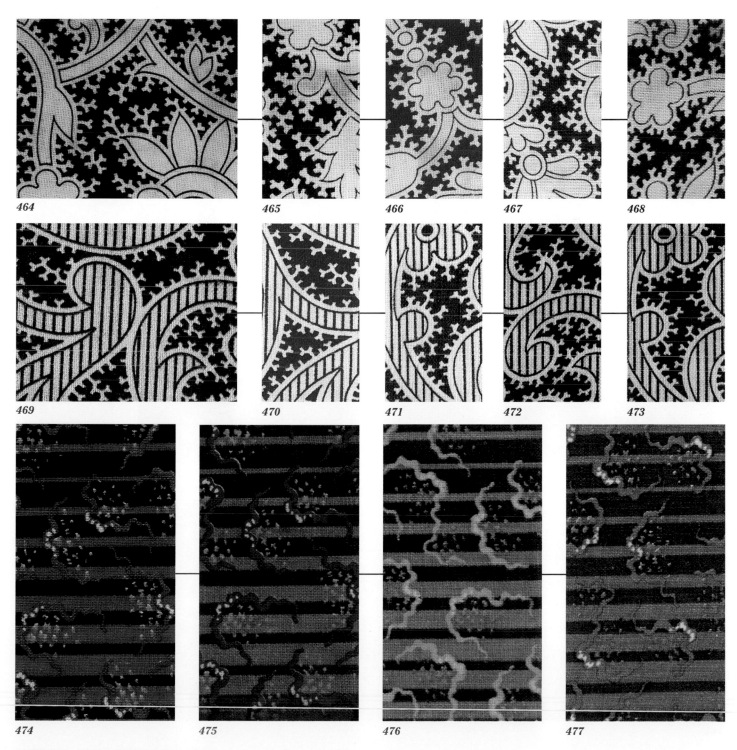

464

465

466

467

468

469

470

471

472

473

474

475

476

477

478–488 1900–1925

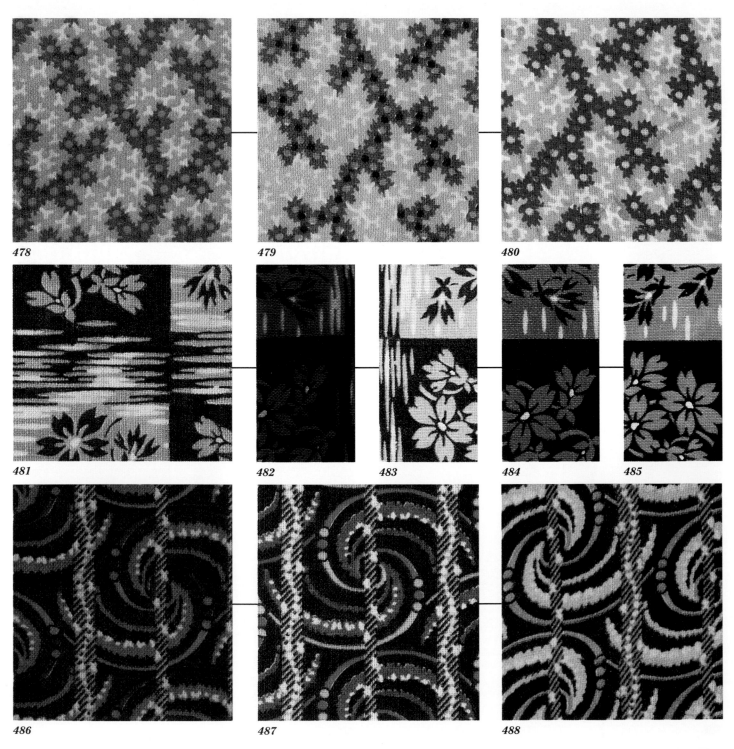

478

479

480

481

482

483

484

485

486

487

488

Calico Man – The Manny Kopp Fabric Collection

489–500 1900–1925

489

490

491

492

493

494

495

496

497

498

499

500

Bobbie A. Aug & Sharon Newman

CALICO

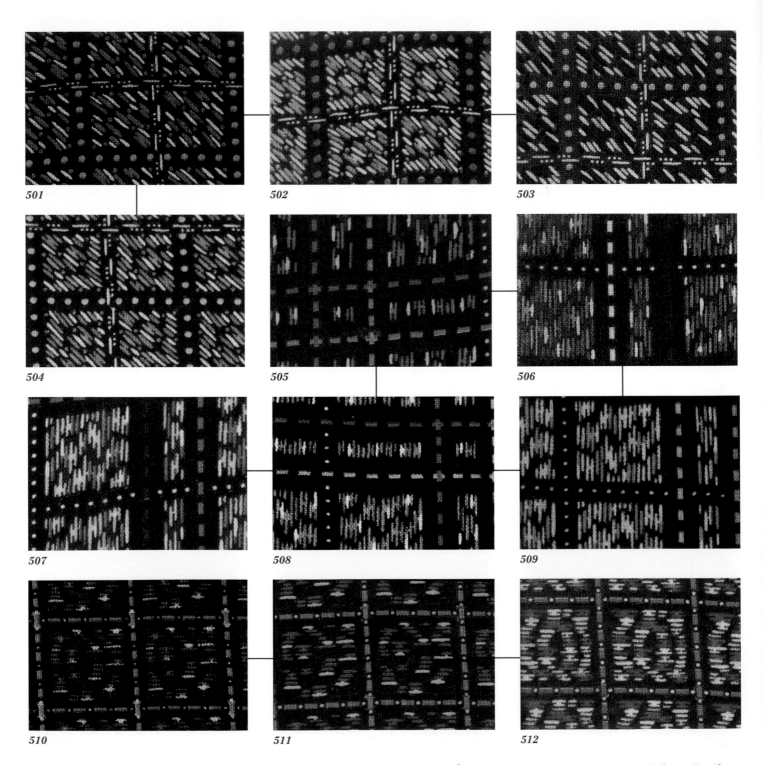

501

502

503

504

505

506

507

508

509

510

511

512

513–525 1900–1925

513

514

515

516

517

518

519

520

521

522

523

524

525

Bobbie A. Aug & Sharon Newman

CALICO

526–535 1900–1925

526

527

528

529

530

531

532

533

534

535

536–549 1900–1925

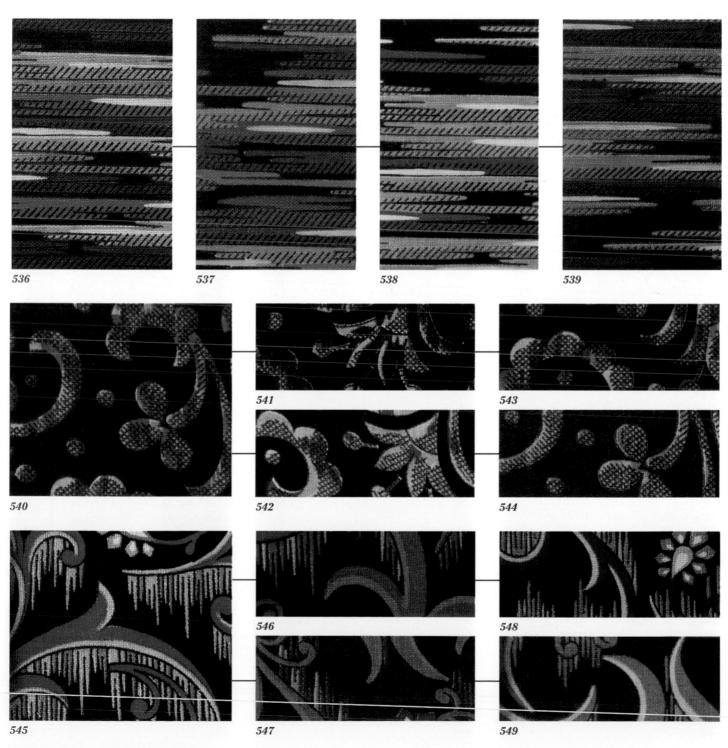

536

537

538

539

540

541

542

543

544

545

546

547

548

549

Bobbie A. Aug & Sharon Newman

CALICO

550

551

552

553

554

555

556

557

558

559

560

561

562–573 1900–1925

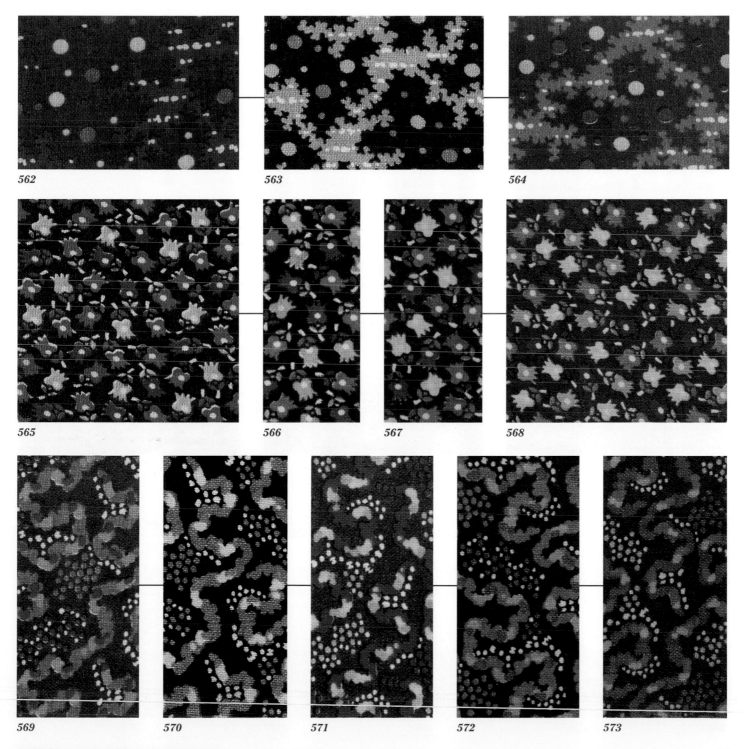

562

563

564

565

566

567

568

569

570

571

572

573

Bobbie A. Aug & Sharon Newman

CALICO

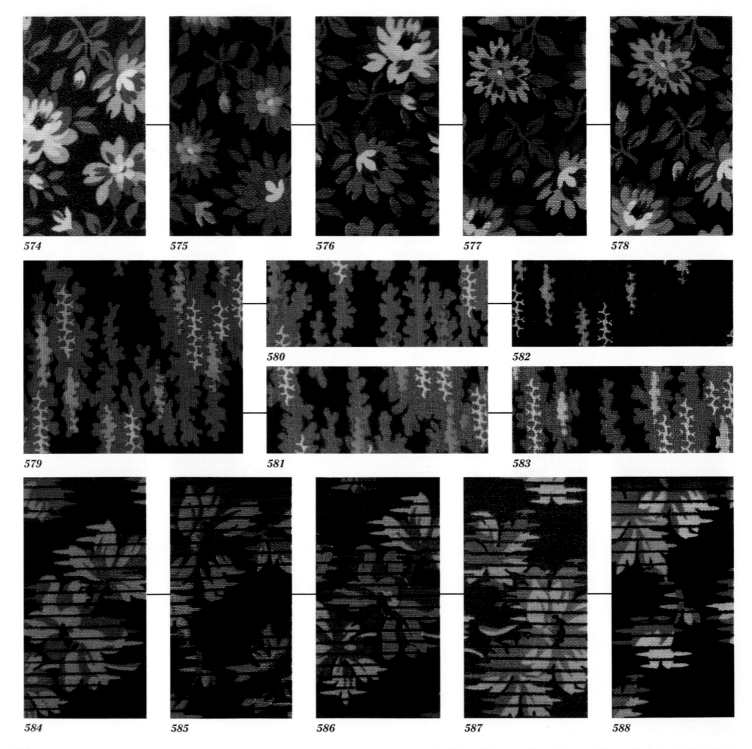

574   575   576   577   578

579   580   582   581   583

584   585   586   587   588

Calico Man – The Manny Kopp Fabric Collection

589–601 1900–1925

589

590

591

592

593

594

595

596

597

598

599

600

601

Bobbie A. Aug & Sharon Newman

CALICO

602–615 1900–1925

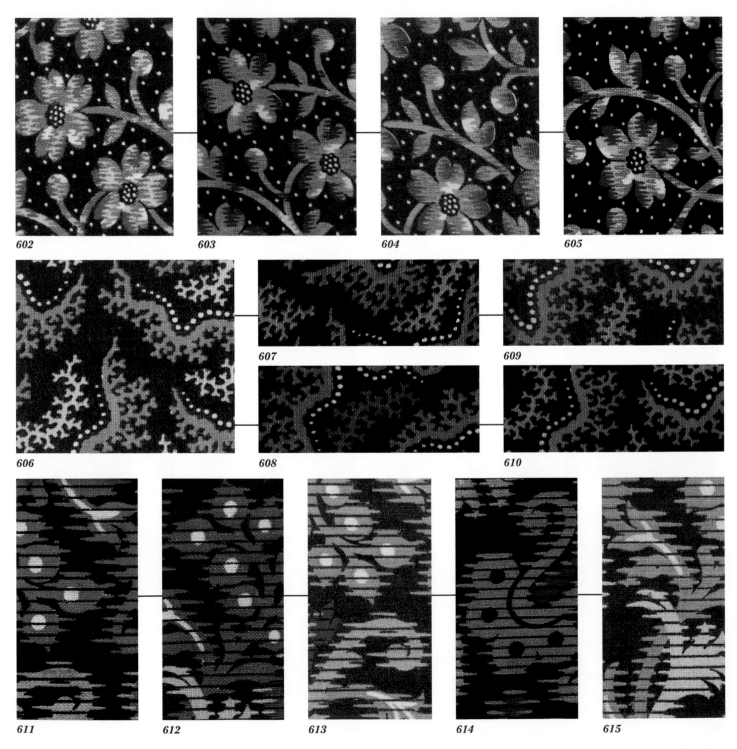

602 603 604 605

606 607 608 609 610

611 612 613 614 615

616–631 1900–1925

616

617

618

619

620

621

622

623

624

625

626

627

628

629

630

631

Bobbie A. Aug & Sharon Newman

CALICO

632–636 1900–1925 (five colorways)

637–638 1900–1925 (two colorways)

639–640 1900–1925 (two colorways)

641–643 1900–1925 (three colorways)

644–646 1900–1925 (three colorways)

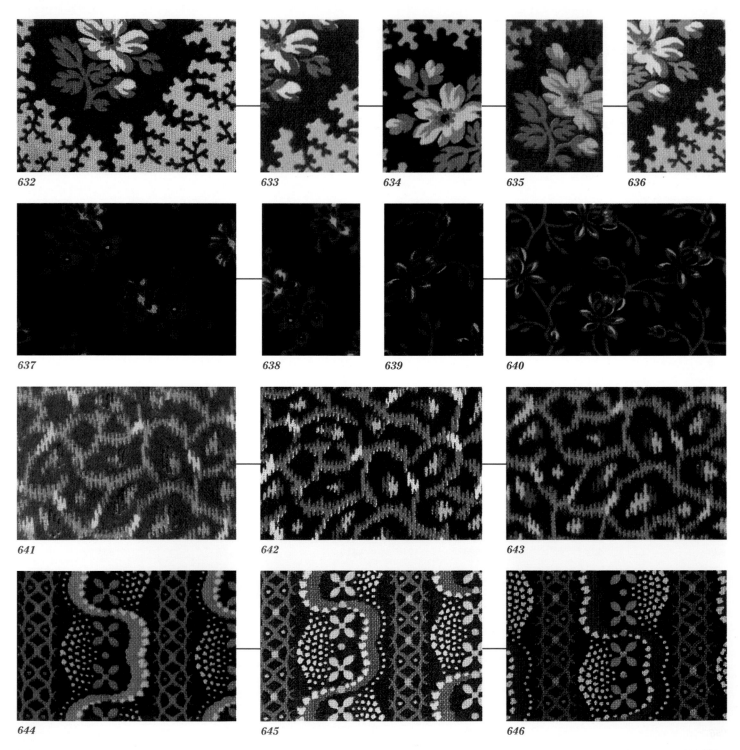

632

633

634

635

636

637

638

639

640

641

642

643

644

645

646

647–658 1900–1925

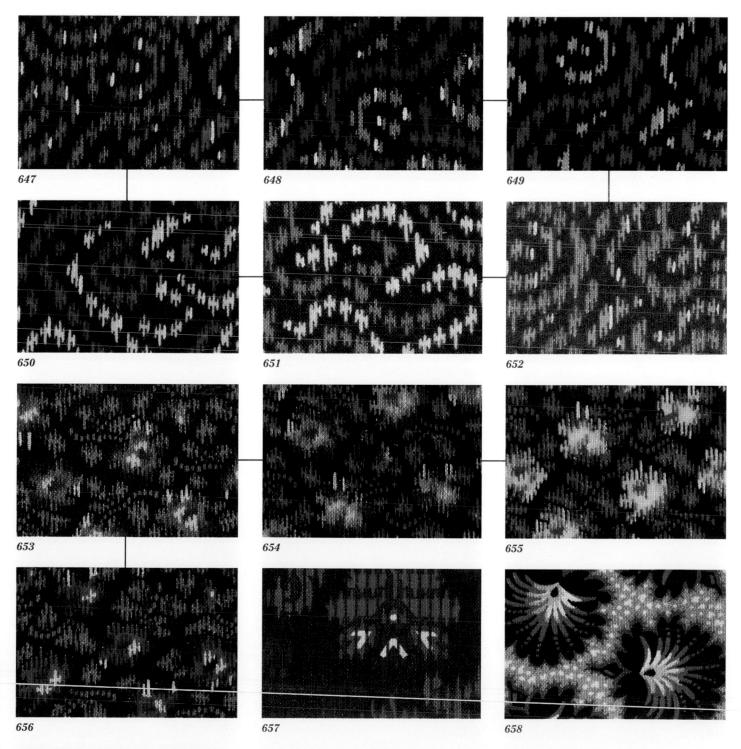

647

648

649

650

651

652

653

654

655

656

657

658

Bobbie A. Aug & Sharon Newman

CALICO

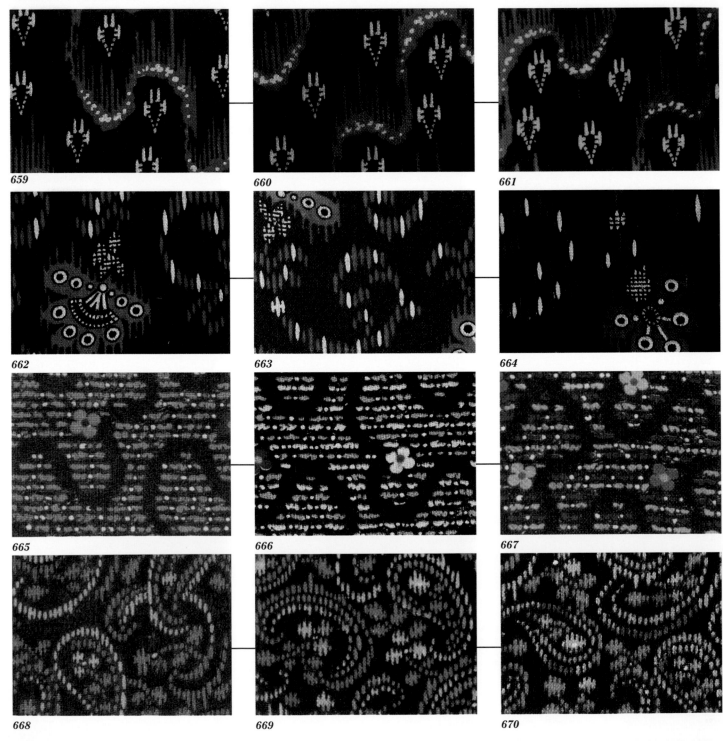

659

660

661

662

663

664

665

666

667

668

669

670

671–681 ca. 1900

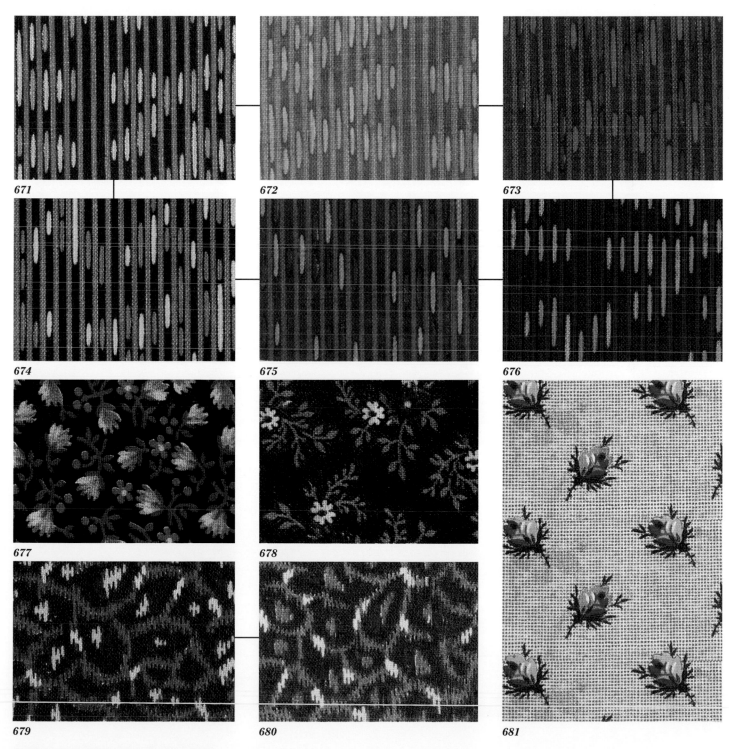

671

672

673

674

675

676

677

678

679

680

681

Bobbie A. Aug & Sharon Newman

CALICO

682–686   1900–1925 (five colorways)

687   Garibaldi-style robe print, 1875–1900

688   Garibaldi-style robe print, 1875–1900

682

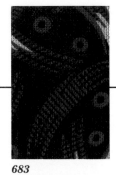

683

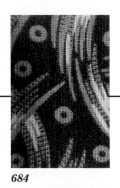

684

685

686

687

688

689   Garibaldi-style robe prints, 1875–1900

690–694   1875–1900

689

690

691

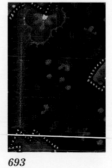

692

693

694

Bobbie A. Aug & Sharon Newman

CALICO

695–697 1875–1900 (three colorways)
698–703 ca. 1900
704–705 ca. 1900 (two colorways)
    706 ca. 1900

695

696

697

698

699

700

701

702

703

704

705

706

707–709 1900–1925 (three colorways). It is possible that 707 and 708 are the same fabric, each from a different dye run.

710–714 ca. 1900

715 1875–1900

716 ca. 1900

707

708

709

710

711

712

713

714

715

716

CALICO

717–719 1875–1900
720 ca. 1900

717

718

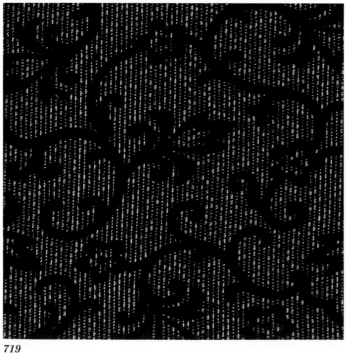

719

720

721–722 ca. 1900

723 1875–1900

724–725 1888–1900

726–727 1900–1925

728–729 Companion prints, ca. 1900

721

722

723

724

725

726

727

728

729

CALICO

730–34 1875–1900
735–736 ca. 1900
737–738 1875–1900

730

731

732

733

734

735

736

737

738

739–741 Companion prints, ca. 1900

742–743 Madder prints, 1875–1900

744 1875–1900

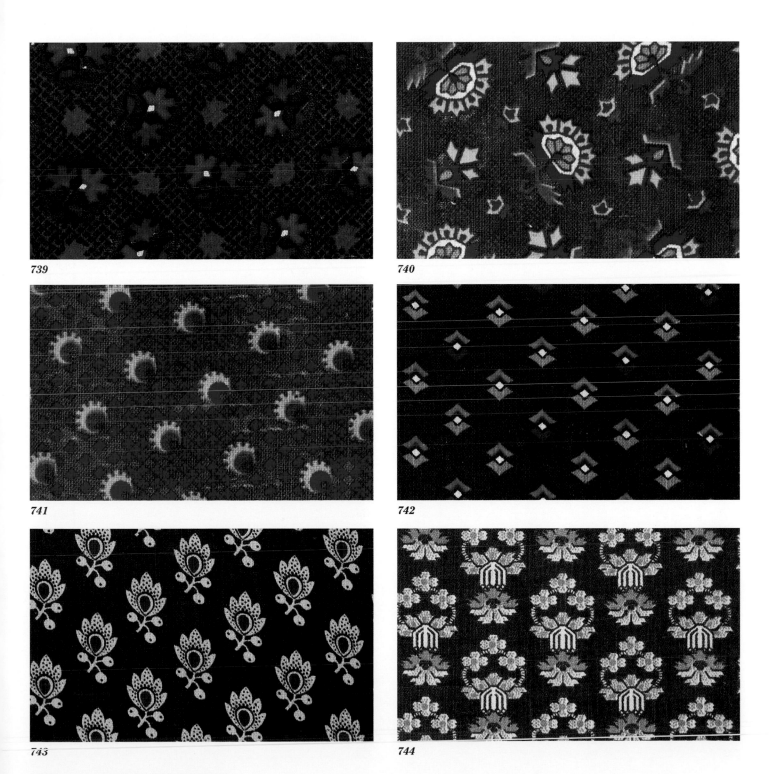

739

740

741

742

743

744

Bobbie A. Aug & Sharon Newman

CALICO

745 1900–1925
746 1850–1875
747 1875–1900
748 ca. 1900
749 1900–1925
750 ca. 1900

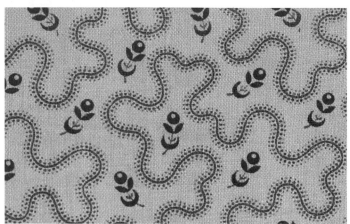

745

746

747

748

749

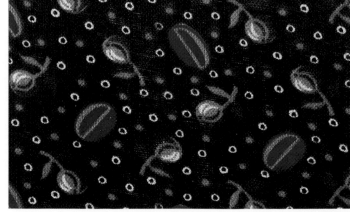

750

751–753 Companion prints, ca. 1900

754 1900–1925

755–757 1900–1925 (three colorways)

751

752

753

754

755

756

757

Bobbie A. Aug & Sharon Newman

CALICO

758   ca. 1900

759–763   Companion prints, ca. 1900 (five colorways)

764–769   Companion prints, ca. 1900 (six colorways). It is possible that 766 and 768 are the same fabric, each from a different dye run.

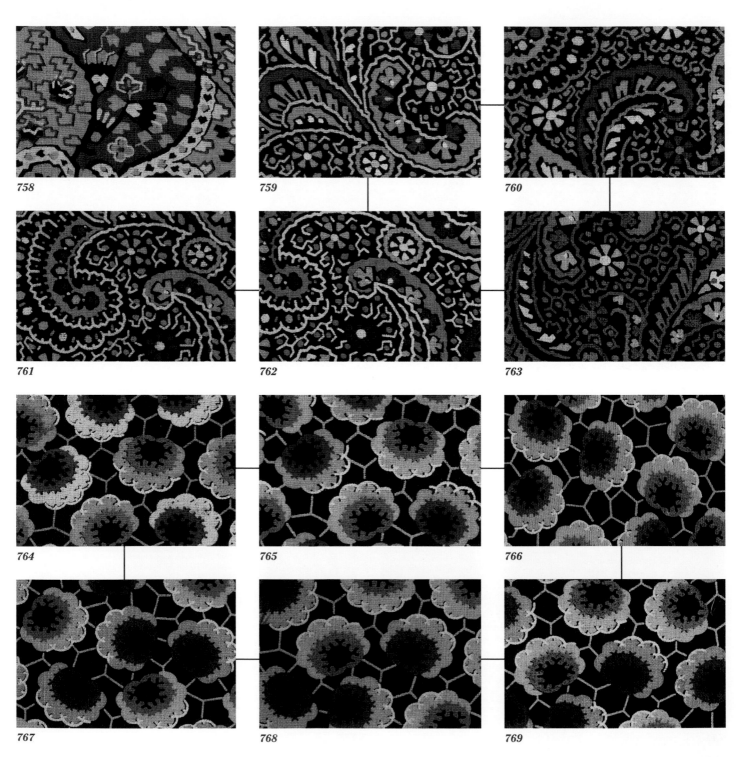

758

759

760

761

762

763

764

765

766

767

768

769

770–774 Companion pieces, ca. 1900 (five colorways)

775–779 Companion pieces, ca. 1900 (five colorways)

780–782 Neats, 1900–1925

783–784 Neats, 1900–1925 (two colorways)

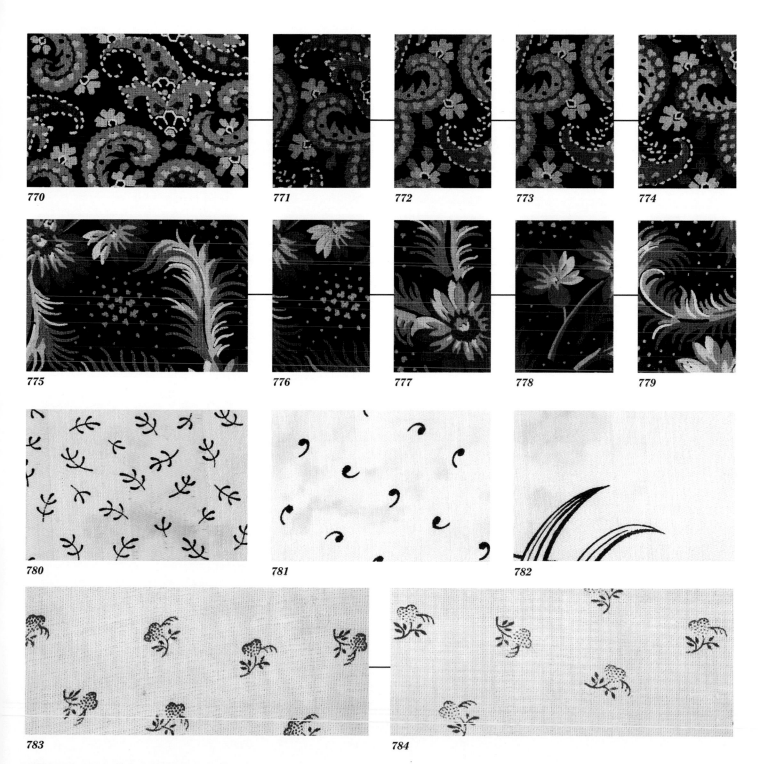

770

771

772

773

774

775

776

777

778

779

780

781

782

783

784

Bobbie A. Aug & Sharon Newman

CALICO

785–786   1900–1925
787–788   ca. 1900 (two colorways)
789–790   1900–1925 (two colorways)

785

787

786

788

789

790

791–793 Companion prints, 1850–1875

794–799 Companion prints, 1900–1925

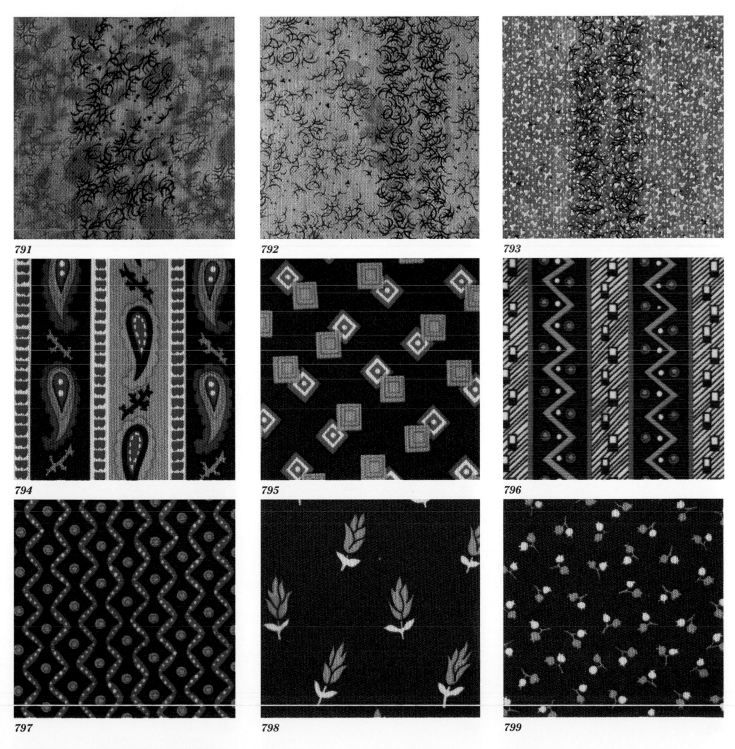

791

792

793

794

795

796

797

798

799

Bobbie A. Aug & Sharon Newman

CALICO

800–802 "Passaic W Challie," Style 7365, 1926 (three colorways)

803–804 Discharge prints, 1875–1900 (two colorways)

805 Black stipple print, 1875–1900

806 1900–1925

807–808 Companion prints, 1900–1925

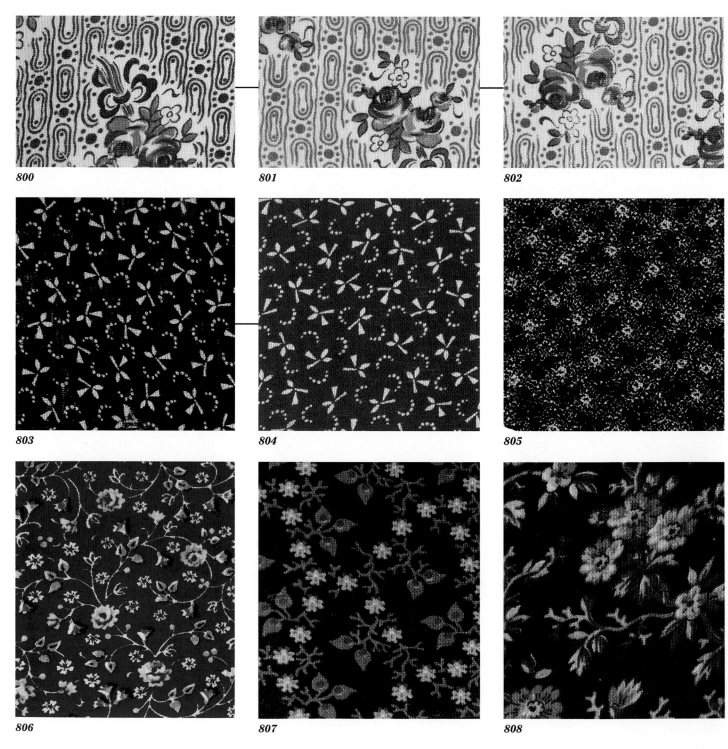

800

801

802

803

804

805

806

807

808

809–812 1900–1925
813 1875–1900

809

810

811

812

813

CALICO

814-815 1900–1925

816-818 1850–1875 (later reproduced in the twentieth century)

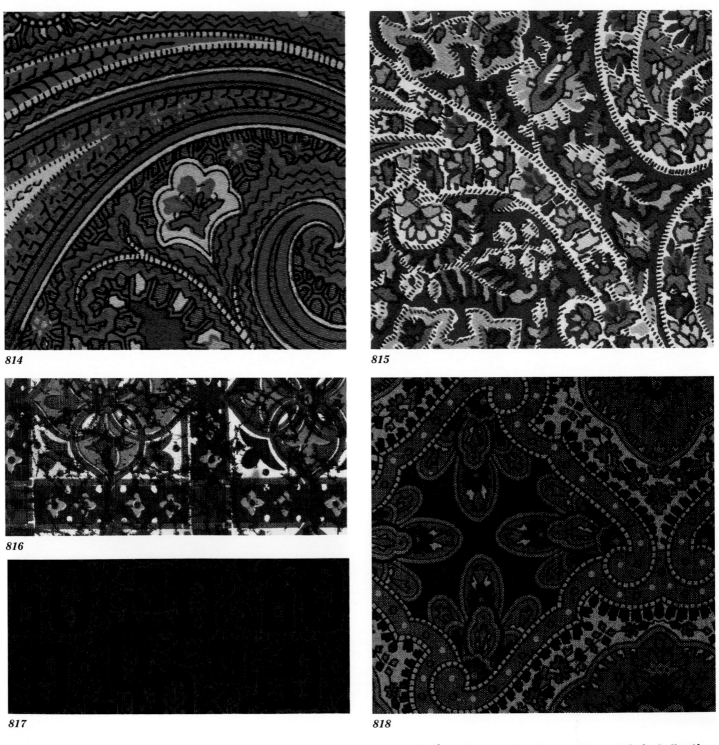

814

815

816

817

818

Calico Man – The Manny Kopp Fabric Collection

819 Floral printed paisley, 1875–1900

820–821 Border prints, ca. 1900

822 ca. 1900

823 Feather twill, 1875–1900

824 Seersucker print, 1900–1925

825 Chain print, 1875–1900

819

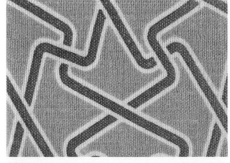

820

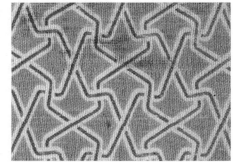

821

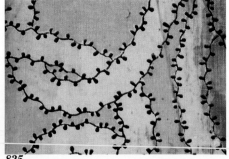

822

823

824

825

Bobbie A. Aug & Sharon Newman

CHECKS

It seems as though checks have been around forever and have indeed been produced since the first half of the nineteenth century. The popularity of this particular design style is possibly due to the variety of check patterns available. Checks are produced when the stripes in a plaid end in squares. Stripes of the same width result in a gingham-check pattern. Another check pattern resembles windowpanes. Any style of check could be achieved by either weaving the pattern into the cloth or by printing the pattern onto the surface of the cloth after it has been woven. Checks remain popular today.

01   ca. 1900
02–04   1900–1925 (three colorways)
05–09   1900–1925 (five colorways)

01

02

03

04

05   06   07   08   09

Plaid is a square or rectangular arrangement of stripes, most often horizontal and vertical, with the stripes intersecting frequently at right angles. Weaving plaid patterns could easily have originated by accident. A weaver, not having enough thread of the warp (vertical) color, may have resorted to using a different thread for the weft (horizontal) threads, thus resulting in a plaid pattern.

The printing detail was so sophisticated that often the printed pattern was difficult to distinguish from a woven design. The color palette and scale of plaids changed along with other prints to reflect popular trends in the home decorating and fashion industries.

01	1875–1900
02	Fine woven plaid, ca. 1800
03	Blotch-printed plaid, 1912
04–07	1900–1925

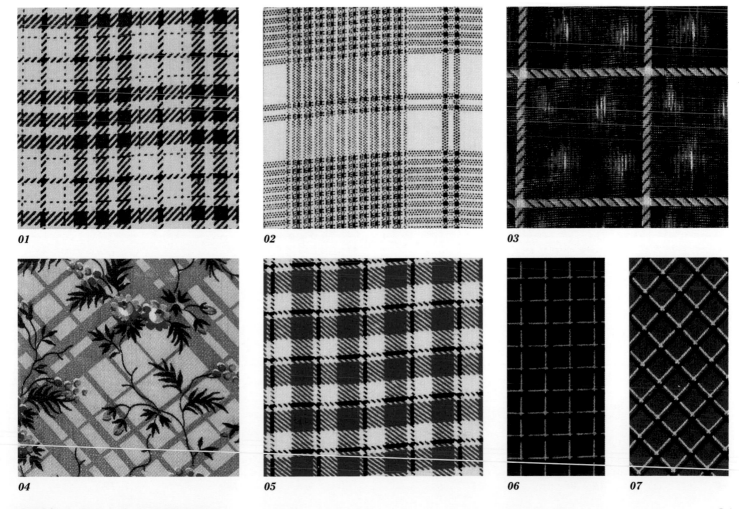

01

02

03

04

05

06

07

PLAIDS

08   Micro check, 1900–1925

09   1850–1875

10   1875–1900

11–14   1900–1925 (four colorways)

15–19   Twill weaves, 1900–1925 (five variations)

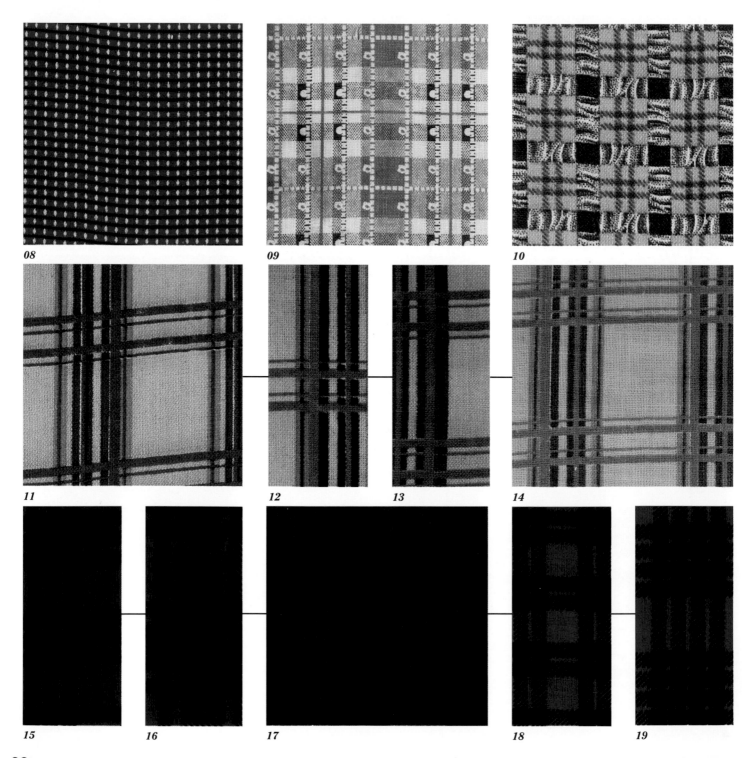

08

09

10

11

12

13

14

15

16

17

18

19

Calico Man – The Manny Kopp Fabric Collection

Stripes are most frequently printed vertically, particularly for clothing designs because the vertical stripes have a slimming effect. Shirting stripes are the familiar narrow stripes found in the last two decades of the nineteenth century and the first two decades of the twentieth century. Sometimes the appearance of a stripe is created simply by small figures such as flowers, leaves, or other characters, printed in vertical or horizontal rows.

Stripes have been woven into wool and printed in cotton in nearly every decade. French stripes of deep, rich colors were popular in 1810 and 1820. Not long after, undulating or eccentric stripes were created accidentally, then continued in the early nineteenth century. Stripes with the appearance of texture were often printed to look like woven designs during the 1890s. At the end of World War II, stripes were popular again for both women's and men's clothing.

01–02　1875–1900 (two colorways)

03–06　Madder stripe, 1875–1900 (four colorways)

07　Madder stripe, 1875–1900

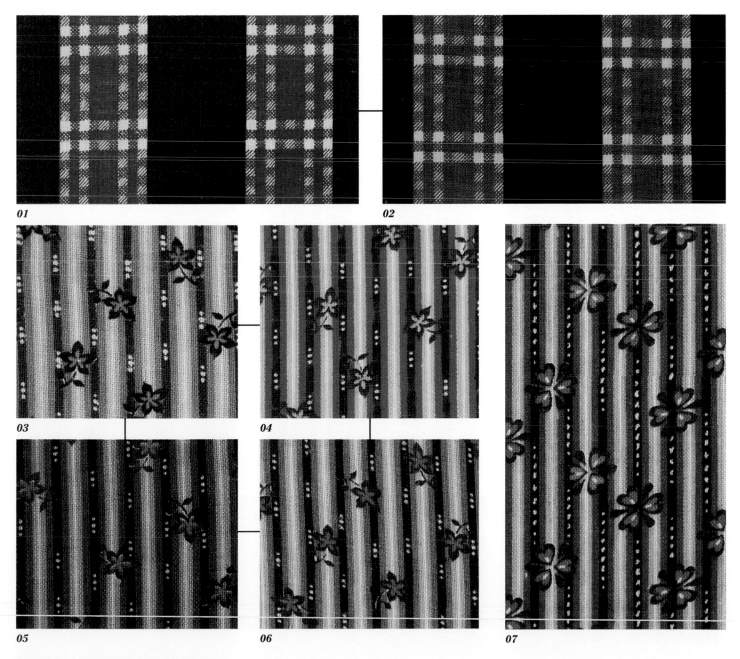

01

02

03

04

05

06

07

STRIPES

08–10 "Cotton Calico" ticking stripes, 1875–1900 (three colorways)

11–13 Ticking, 1900–1925 (three colorways)

14–15 Ticking, 1900–1925

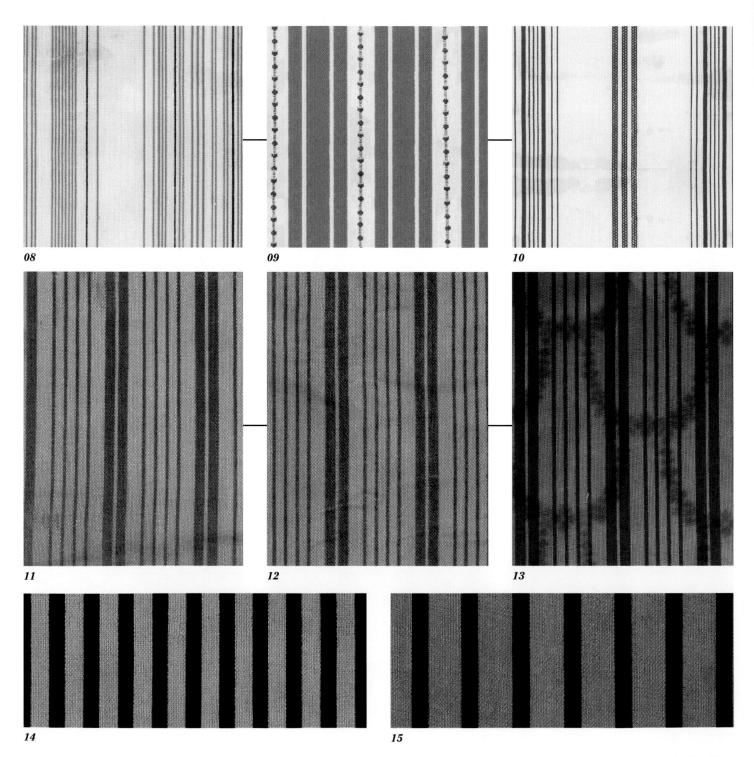

08

09

10

11

12

13

14

15

16–18   1875–1900 (three colorways)
19   1875–1900
20   1875–1900
21   1875–1900
22   1875–1900

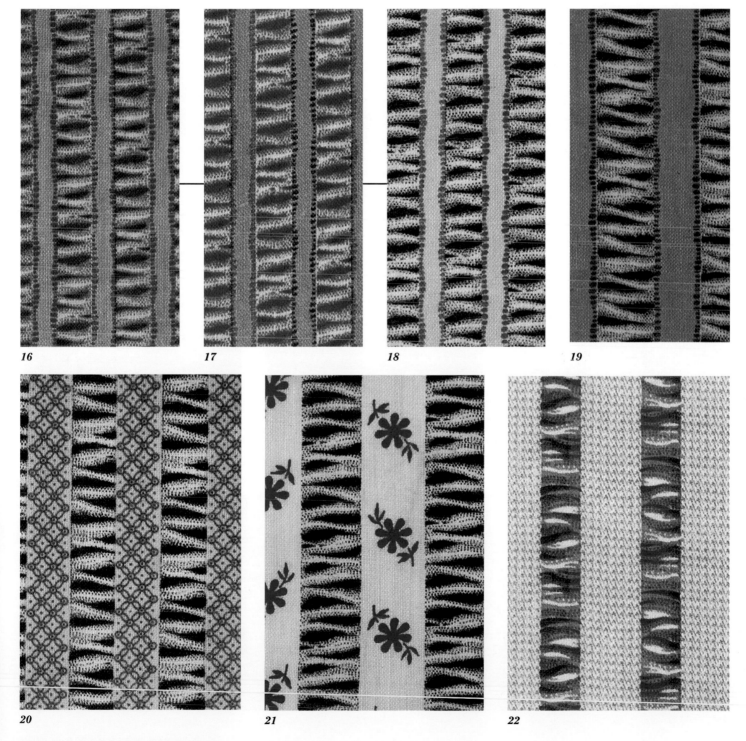

16   17   18   19

20   21   22

STRIPES

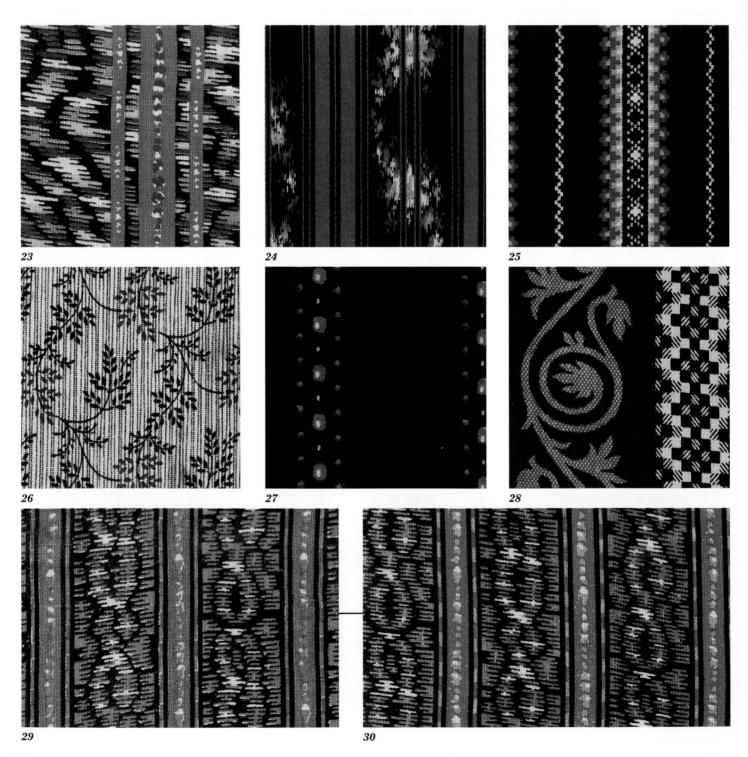

23

24

25

26

27

28

29

30

Calico Man – The Manny Kopp Fabric Collection

31–32 Lace print border stripe, 1900–1925 (two colorways)

33 1900–1925

34 1875–1900

35–36 1900–1925 (two colorways)

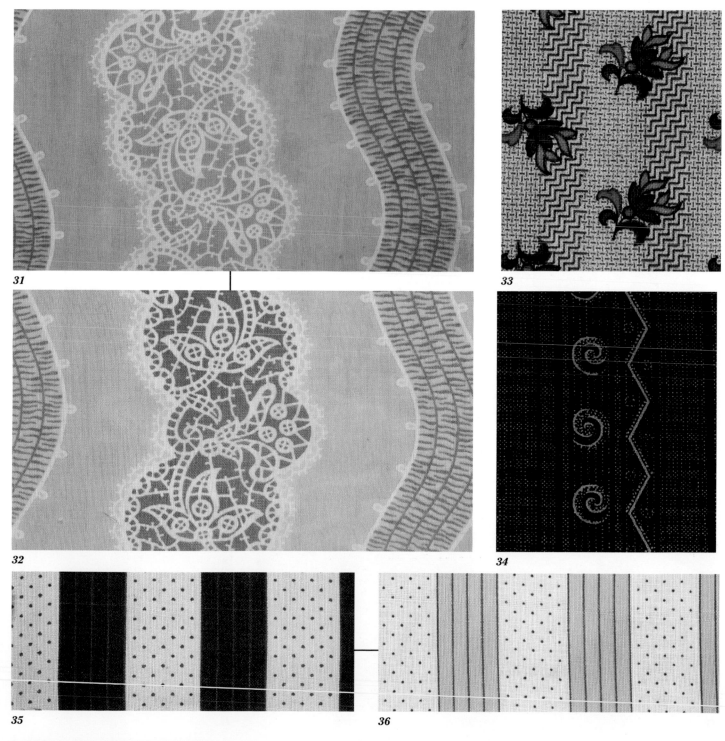

31

32

33

34

35

36

Bobbie A. Aug & Sharon Newman

STRIPES

37

38

39

40

41

42

43

44

45

46

47

48–50   1900–1925
51–52   1875–1900 (two colorways)
53–54   1900–1925
55–57   1900–1925 (three colorways)

48

49

50

51

52

53

54

55

56

57

STRIPES

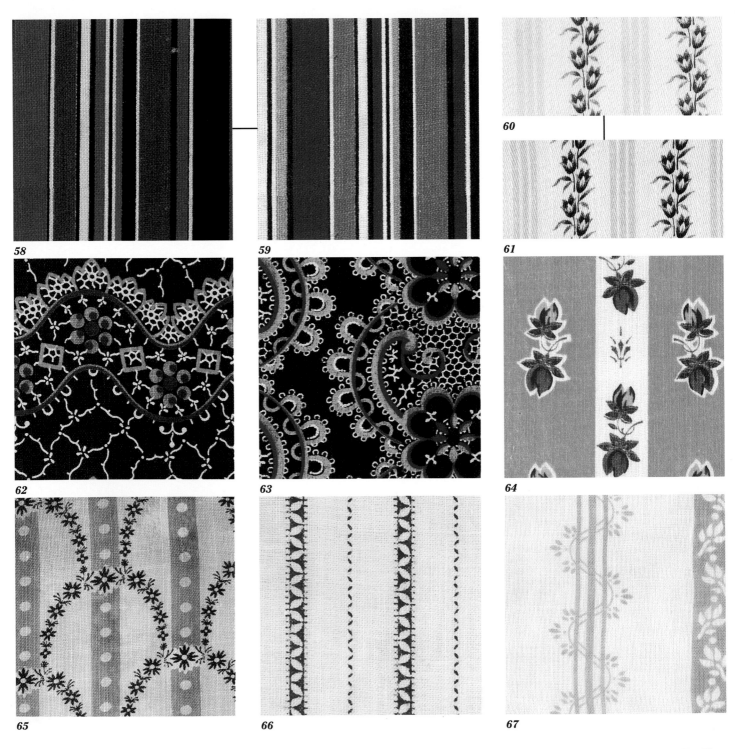

58

59

60

61

62

63

64

65

66

67

68

69

70

71

72

73

74

75

76

77

78

79

CONVERSATIONAL PRINTS

Sometimes called character prints, these designs were popular from the early toiles printed with large-scale landscapes and pictorials with people engaged in daily activity to the somewhat simple and widely spaced characters of the twentieth century. Probably the most traditional are the small to medium prints depicting children at play, sports equipment such as tennis racquets and riding crops, and those that include insects, dogs, and cats, along with objects such as horseshoes and nails. By the early 1950s, their popularity declined.

01 Noah's Ark animals, 1850–1875
02 Drafting tools, 1875–1900
03 Oriental figures, 1875–1900
04 Tiny horseshoes, 1850–1875
05 Rising sun and stars in geometric square, 1875–1900
06 Horseshoes and whip, 1875–1900

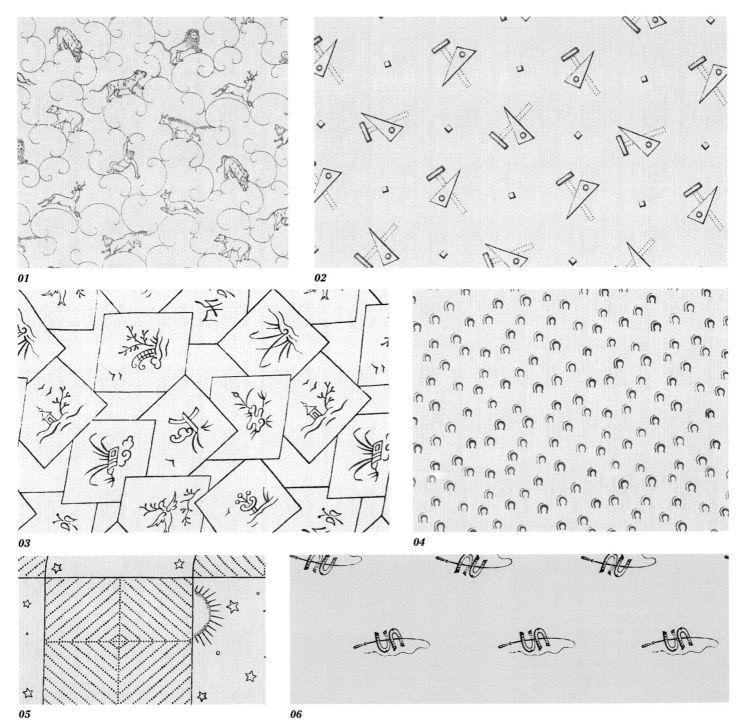

01

02

03

04

05

06

07 French steel mills engravings, 1850–1875
08 Wheel and axle, 1875–1900
09 Stick pins and stars, 1875–1900
10 Horseshoes, 1875–1900
11 Fishing bobbers, 1875–1900

12 Hearts and clubs stick pins, 1875–1900
13 Card flags and hearts, 1875–1900
14 World map in geometric setting, 1875–1900
15 Floating buttons, 1875–1900

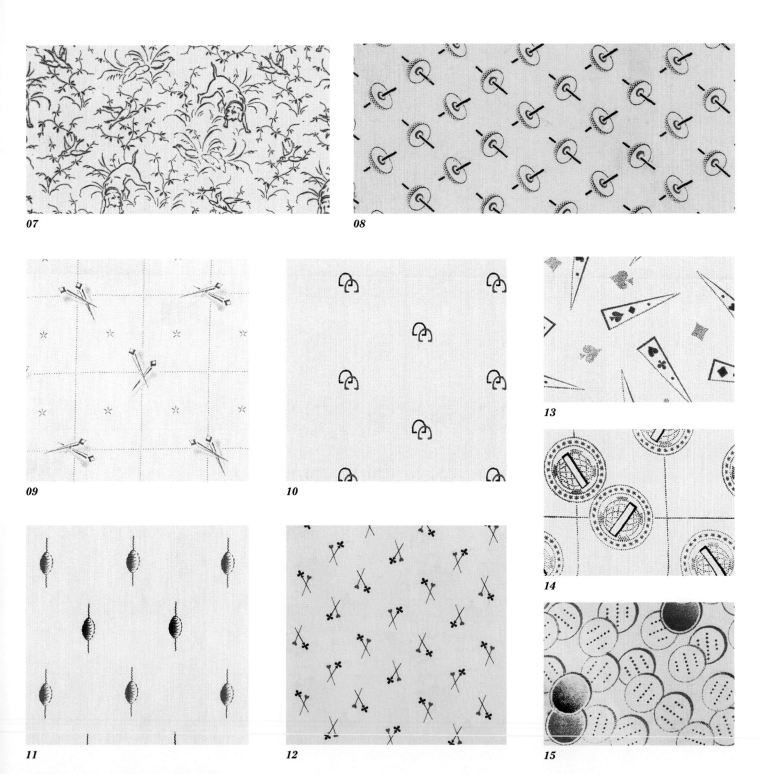

07

08

09

10

13

14

11

12

15

CONVERSATIONAL PRINTS

16 Horses' heads in stripe, 1875–1900
17 Rider and whip, 1875–1900
18 Circles with card symbols, 1875–1900
19 Eye screws, 1875–1900
20 Carpenters' tools, 1875–1900

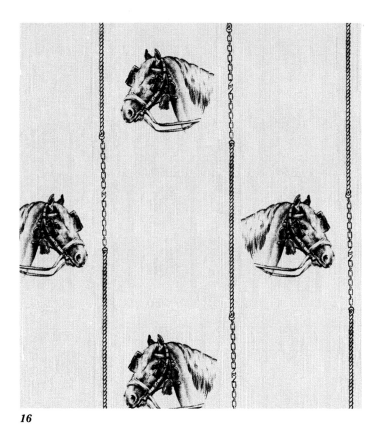

16

17

18

19

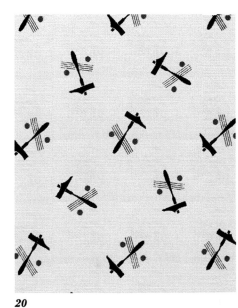

20

21 Anchors and dots, blue and red, 1850–1875

22 Dogs' heads in red, 1875–1900

23 Checkerboard with card motifs, 1875–1900

24 Springs in plaid, 1875–1900

25 Bent nails, 1875–1900

26 Keys, 1875–1900

27 Fleur-de-lis, 1875–1900

21

22

23

24

25

26

27

CONVERSATIONAL PRINTS

28

29

30

31

32

33

34

35

36

37

38–43 Horses, horseheads, horse with rider, cards, scissors, dogs, 1875–1900

44 Bent arrows in blue and red, 1875–1900

45 Horseshoes and flowers, steel mill engravings, 1875–1900

46 Playing cards in red and black, 1875–1900

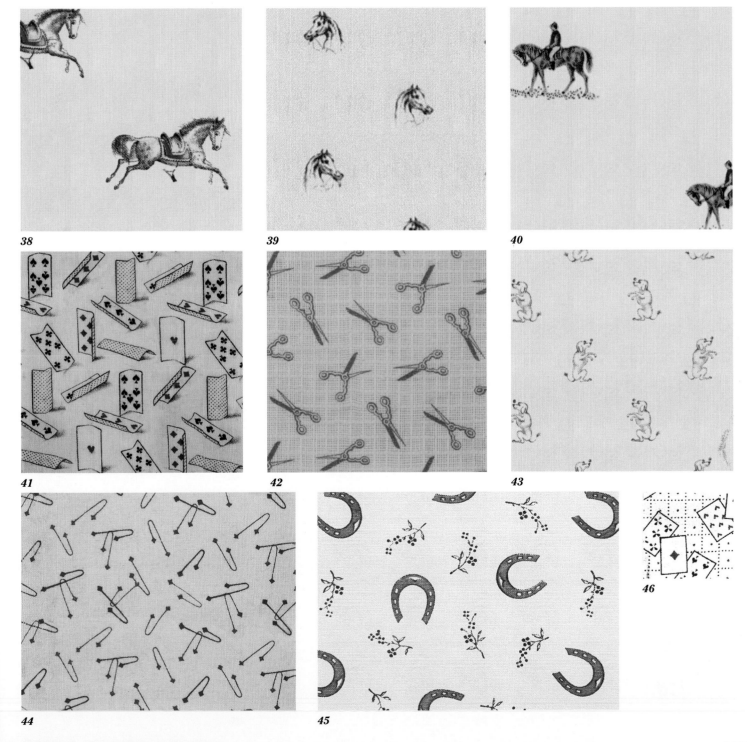

38

39

40

41

42

43

44

45

46

FLANNELETTES

A napping machine was used to create flannels. It consisted of small metal rollers with teeth made of tiny wires. The cotton or wool fabric was passed through the napping machine, where the teeth raised the fibers and created the soft nap of the woven cloth.

01–02   1875–1900
03–04   1900–1925
05   1875–1900

01

02

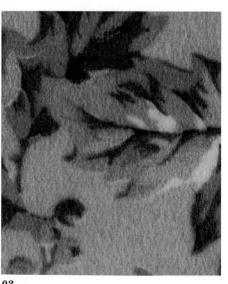

03

04

05

Indigo is one of the oldest and best-known dyes. Egyptian and Indian dyers used the fast blue dye as early as 2500 BC and perhaps even earlier. In the seventeenth and eighteenth centuries AD, expanded trade outlets allowed indigo to be traded universally. Woad was also used to achieve the blue color, but it seems that indigo was more reliable and kinder to the cloth during the dye process. Depending on the length and strength of the dye bath, the color could range from pastel blue to black. Designs created by resist or discharge dyeing techniques made indigo versatile, therefore desirable. Applied as a thick paste to wood blocks made the printing process successful.

In the early nineteenth century, indigo was grown and became an industry in British India, Java, and the islands of the Caribbean. Indigo was the premier dye, and the importation of the chunks or cakes of dye continued. America even had an indigo industry for a while in the third quarter of the nineteenth century.

Early nineteenth-century chemists Ferdinand Runge, William Perkin, and A. von Bayers each played a part through their individual experimentation in the discovery and eventual marketing of aniline or synthetic indigo dye. Synthetic indigo was mass marketed by the late 1890s. This did not immediately affect the exportation of indigo from India, but by the early twentieth century, exportation had declined dramatically.

01   Original painted steel mill engraving, 1874–1875
02   Original painted steel mill engraving, 1874–1875
03   Steel mill engraving, finely detailed, 1875
04   Multicolor indigo with fine-detailed ground, 1810–1820
05   Indigo resist, pre-1825
06   1875–1900

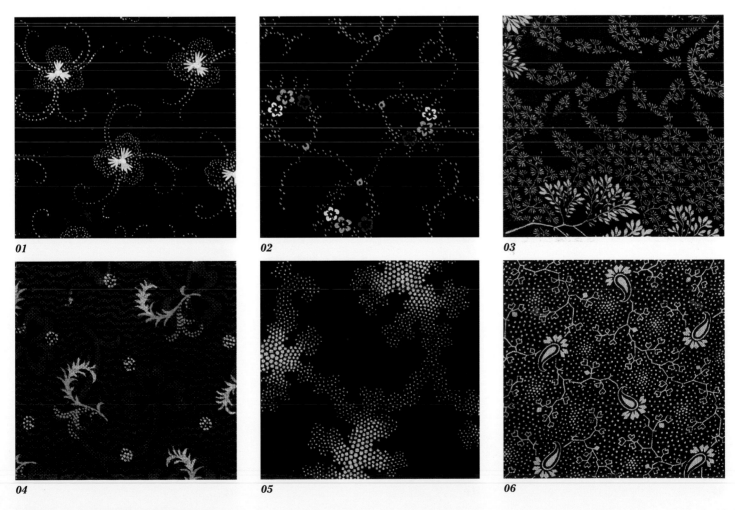

01

02

03

04

05

06

INDIGOES

7–10	1875–1900
11	1800–1825
12	1875–1900
13–14	1810–1830
15	1875–1900

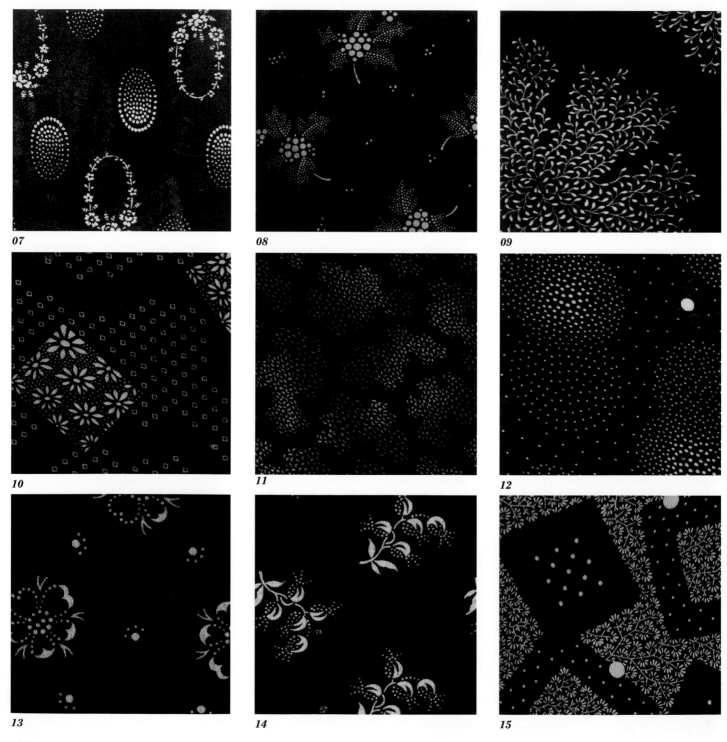

07

08

09

10

11

12

13

14

15

16 Blotch printing resist, 1800–1825
17 French and English, 1875–1900
18 1875–1900
19 Resist printed or discharge printed, 1875–1900
20 Indigo and off-white, 1850–1875

21 1850–1875
22 Regimented motifs, 1825–1850
23–24 1875–1900

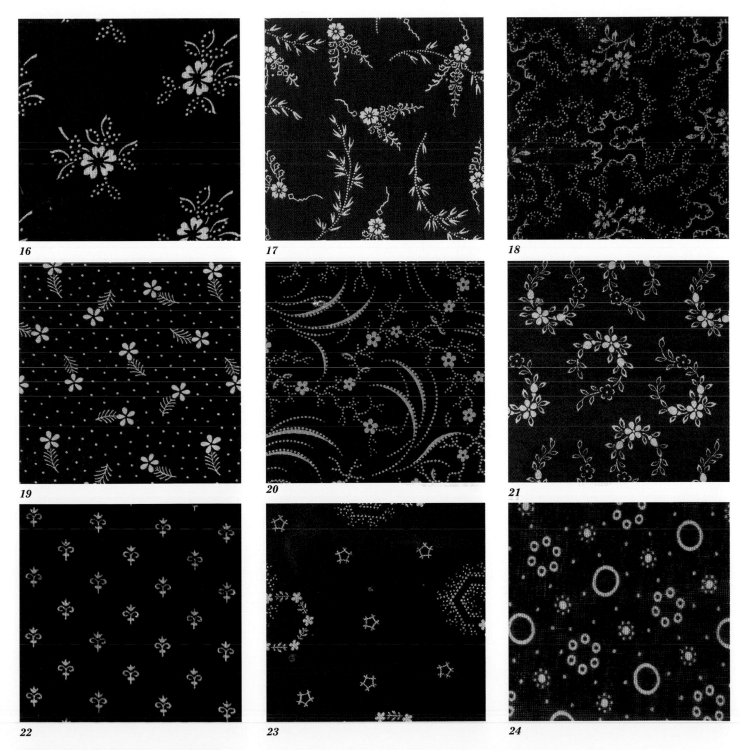

16

17

18

19

20

21

22

23

24

INDIGOES

25

26

27

28

29

30

31

32

33

34	1850–1875
35	1800–1825
36–37	1875–1900
38	1800–1825
39–40	1875–1900
41	1850–1875
42	1875–1900

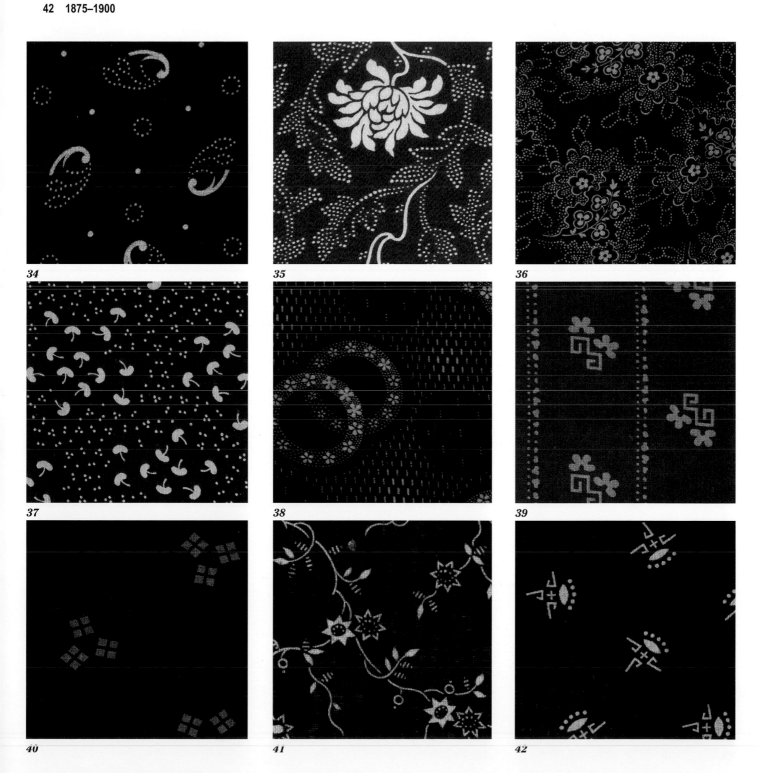

34

35

36

37

38

39

40

41

42

Bobbie A. Aug & Sharon Newman

INDIGOES

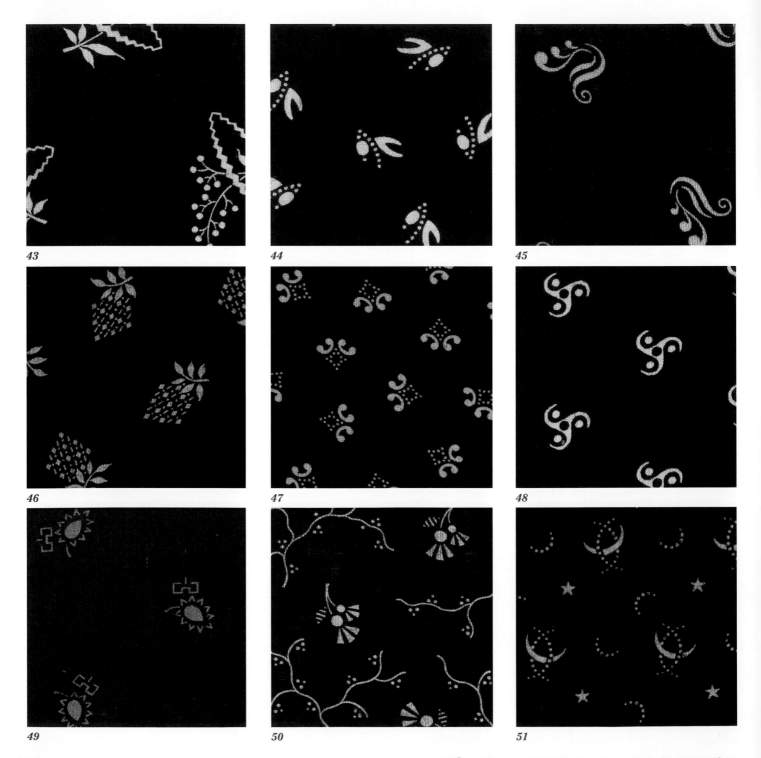

43

44

45

46

47

48

49

50

51

52–53   1900–1925
54–55   1875–1900
   56   Silk, 1875–1900
   57   "1703 Commodius," 1902
   58   "1700 Commit," 1902
59–60   Notation "Salesman's Cards Sent to Poor Brothers' Agents, March 17, 1903" (two colorways)

52

53

54

55

56

57

58

59

60

Bobbie A. Aug & Sharon Newman

LENO WEAVES

Leno weaves contain additional threads woven over the top of a printed design, which add texture and interest, creating a more intricate design.

01–02   1902
03–06   1900–1925 (four colorways)
07–08   1900–1925 (two colorways)
09   1900–1925

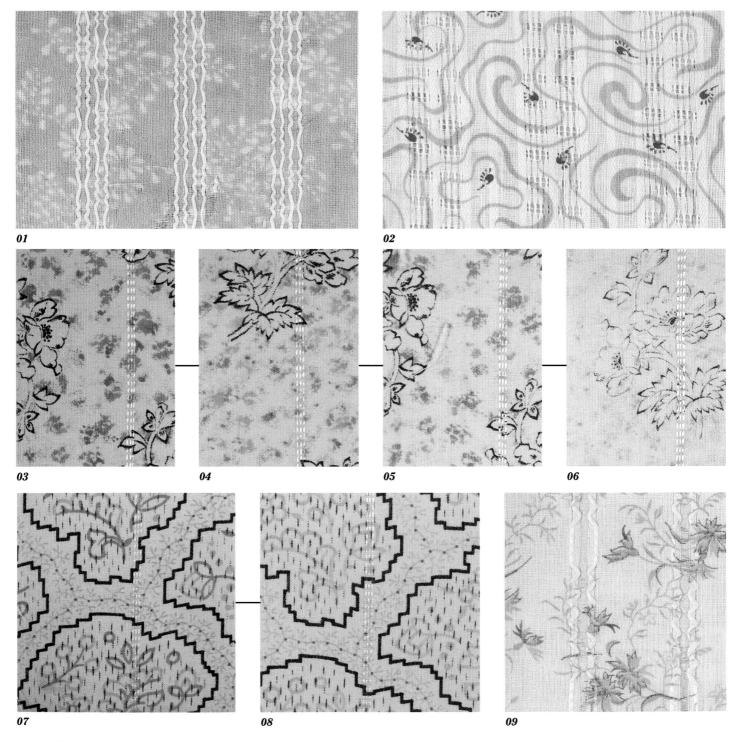

01

02

03

04

05

06

07

08

09

Calico Man – The Manny Kopp Fabric Collection

10–12   1900–1925 (three colorways)

13–14   1900–1925 (two colorways)

15–16   1900–1925 (two colorways)

17–19   1900–1925 (three colorways)

20–21   1900–1925 (two colorways)

22   1900–1925

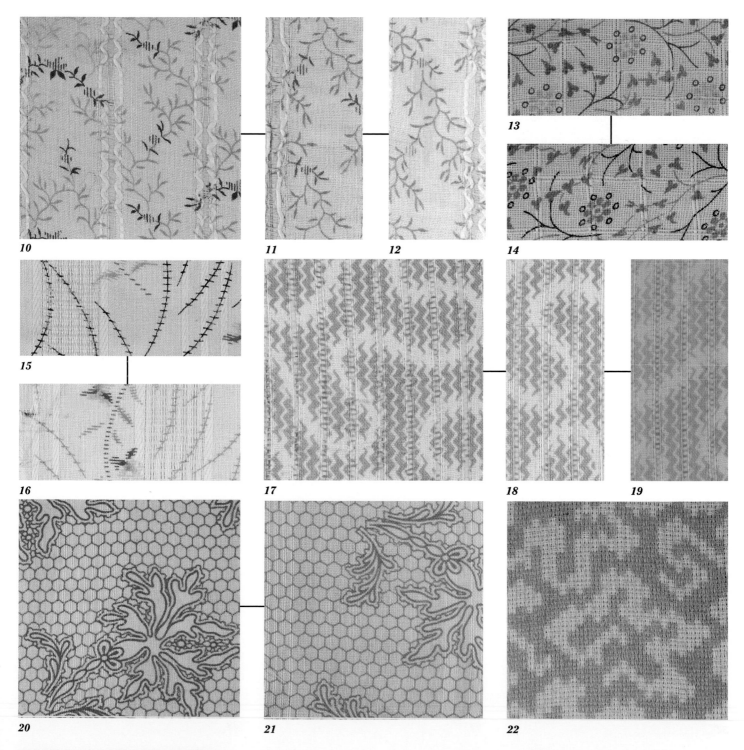

10

11

12

13

14

15

16

17

18

19

20

21

22

LENO WEAVES

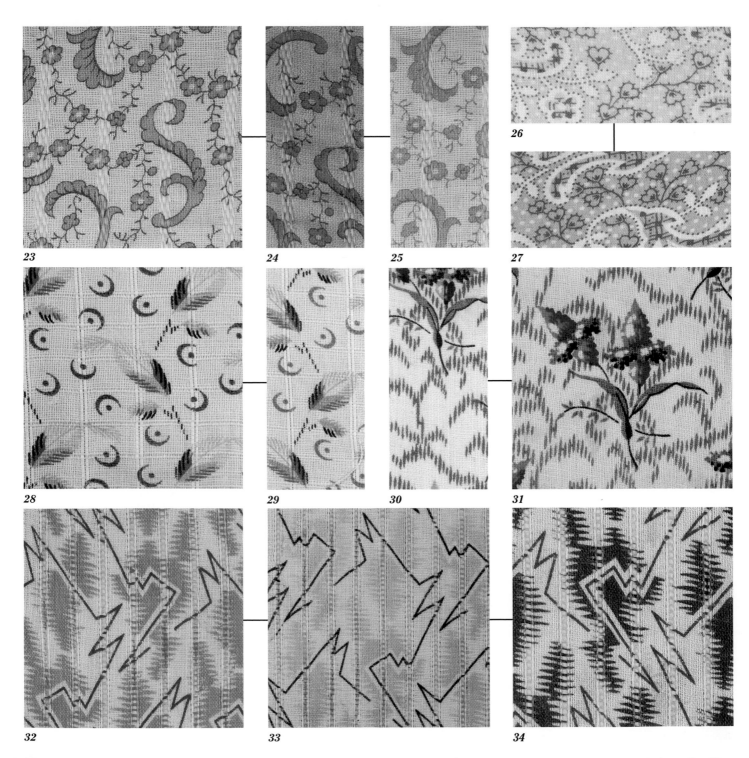

23

24

25

26

27

28

29

30

31

32

33

34

35–36   1900–1925 (two colorways)

37   1900–1925

38–39   1900–1925 (two colorways)

40–41   1900–1925 (two colorways)

42–45   1900–1925 (four colorways)

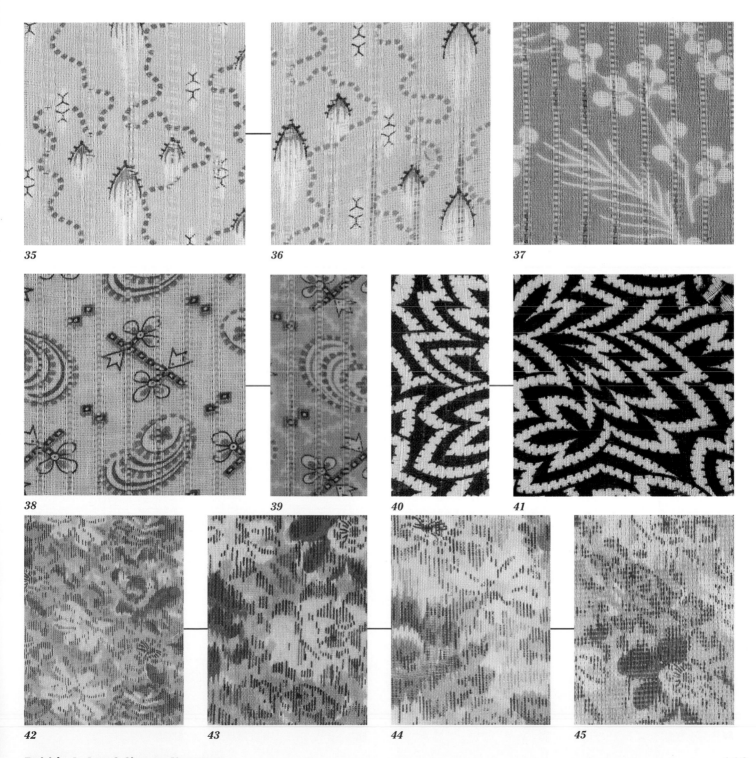

35

36

37

38

39

40

41

42

43

44

45

LENO WEAVES

46–49   1900–1925

50–57   1900–1925 (eight colorways)

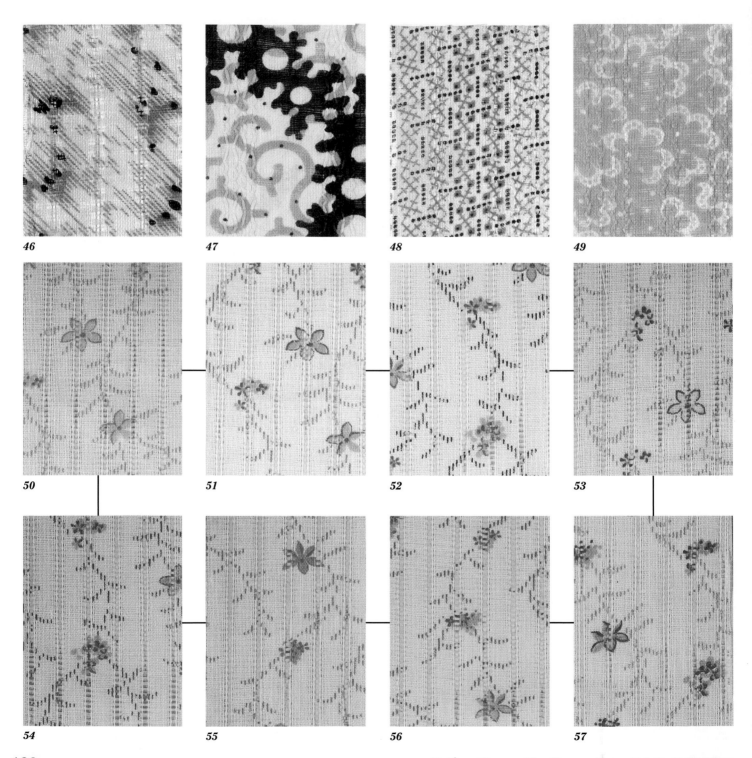

46

47

48

49

50

51

52

53

54

55

56

57

58–59   1900–1925 (two colorways)

60–61   1900–1925 (two colorways)

62–63   1900–1925 (two colorways)

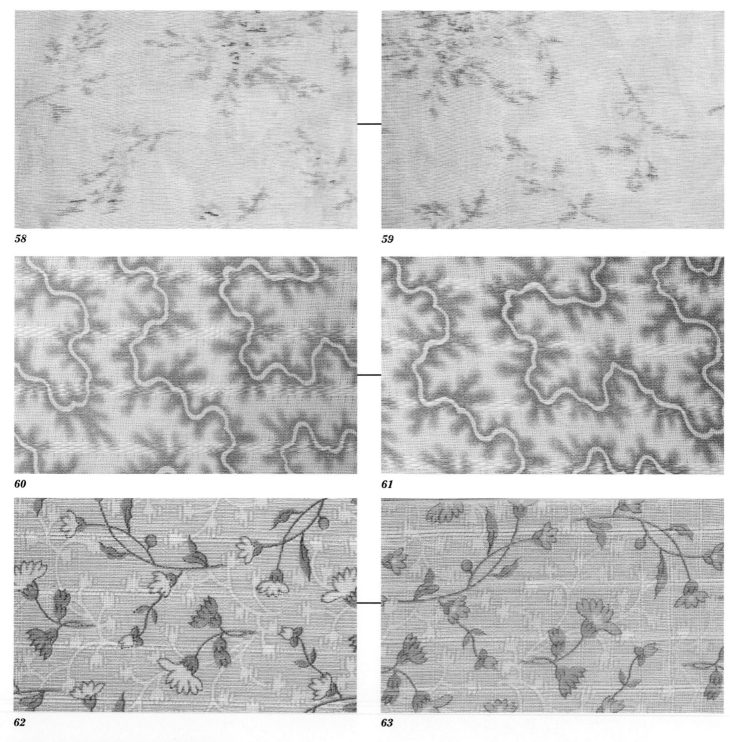

58

59

60

61

62

63

Bobbie A. Aug & Sharon Newman

MOURNING PRINTS

These prints were popular in the last quarter of the nine-teenth century and the first quarter of the twentieth century. They typically consist of a tiny repeated figure or narrow, fine stripe in black printed on a barely visible white ground, sometimes referred to as Shaker grays. Mourning prints were popularized by symbols of Queen Victoria's "mourning" attire popular after the death of her beloved Prince Albert. The Queen remained in mourning for the rest of her life. These prints were considered appropriate for ladies-in-mourning dress goods, but were also popular for general use because they were quite practical in disguising soil.

Dark-colored calicos, in black prints, chocolates, and purples, were often referred to as half-mourning prints. This terms applied to the time of mourning following the first mourning period and style of wearing all black widow's garments.

01–02 1875–1900 (two colorways)]
03–04 1875–1900
    05 Finely engraved ground, ca. 1875
06–09 1875–1900

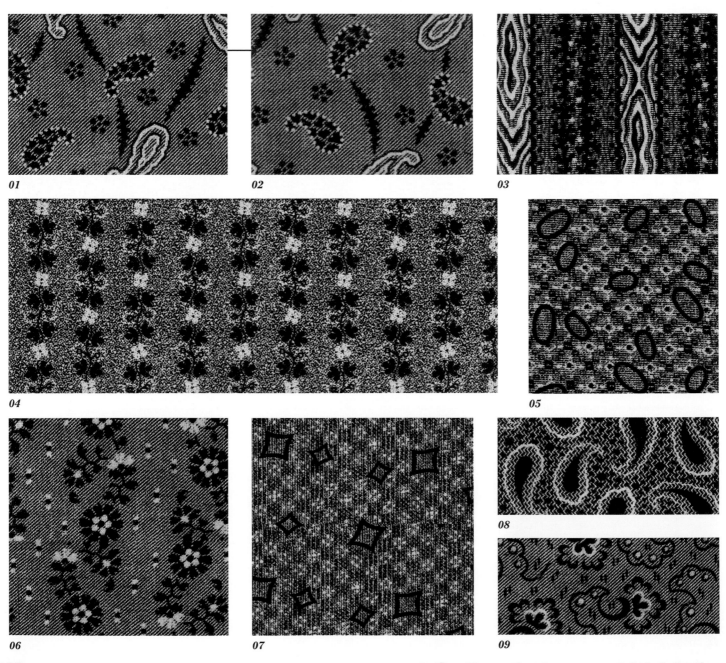

01

02

03

04

05

06

07

08

09

Calico Man – The Manny Kopp Fabric Collection

10–13   1875–1900

14   Finely engraved ground, 1875–1900

15   1875–1900

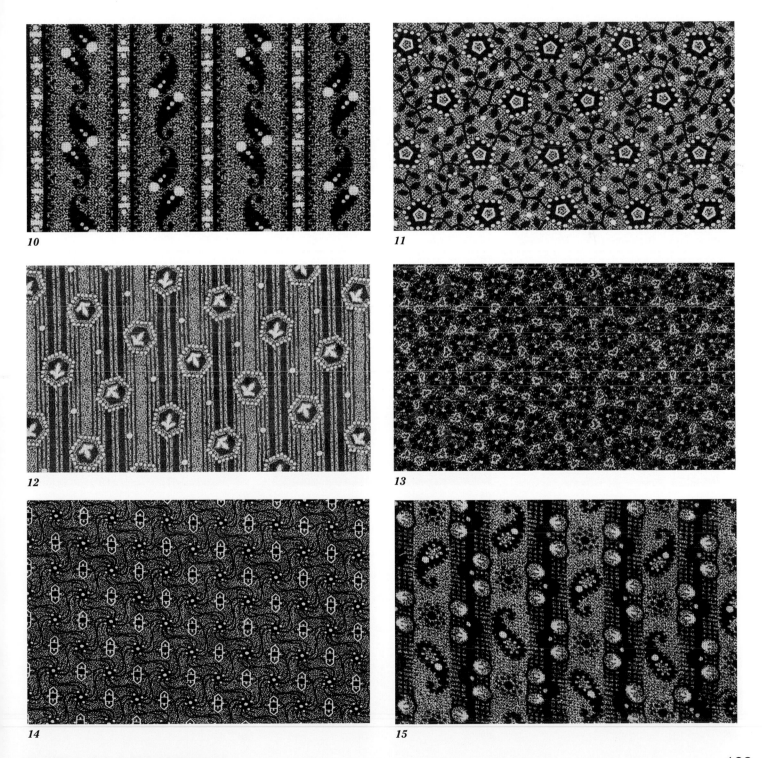

10

11

12

13

14

15

POOR BROTHERS' SALESMAN SAMPLES

All of these swatches were organized into one sample book – obviously one of the original salesman's books. We presume that the sales company or jobber hired to present and sell these fabrics was Poor Brothers. The entire product line was dated 1902.

01–04	Large-scale berry print (four colorways)
05	Checked plaid
06–07	Floral print (two colorways)
08–12	Blue and black stripes (five pieces)

01 02 03 04 05 06 07 08 09 10 11 12

1902

13–14   Large-scale plaid (two colorways)
15   Diamond print
16   Loosely woven printed plaid
17–18   "Electrical" print (two colorways)
19–20   White on claret or lavender and white print (two colorways)

13

14

15

16

17

18

19

20

1902

- 21   Geometric print
- 22   Pink and brown print
- 23   Brown, tan, and teal plaid
- 24–26   Plaid stripe with dots (three colorways)
- 27–29   Celestial white dots on brown, claret, or blue ground (three colorways)

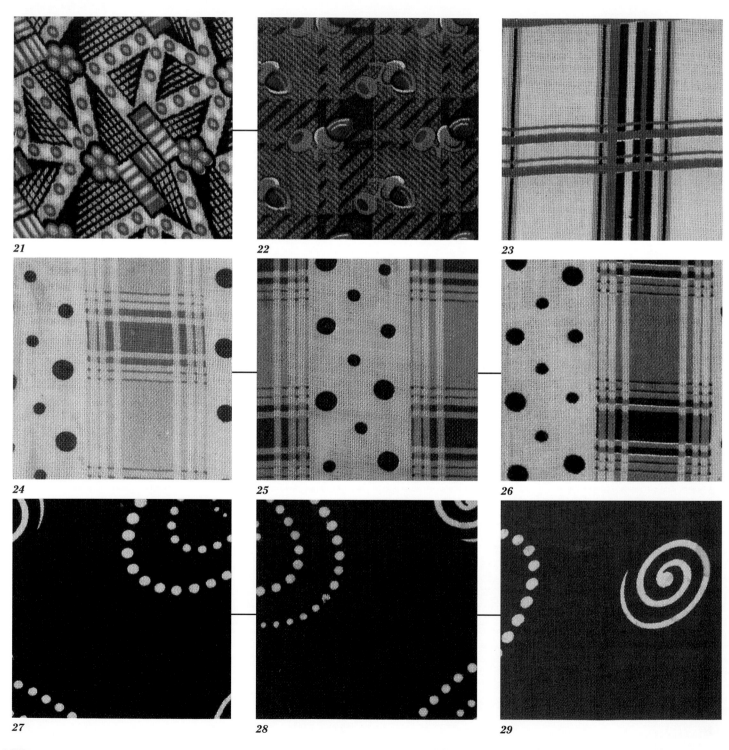

21

22

23

24

25

26

27

28

29

1902

30–31   Floral print (two colorways)

32   Pink and purple floral print on brown

33   Green, black, and pink stripe

34–37   Large floral on light-striped background (four colorways)

30
31
32
33
34
35
36
37

1902

38   Brown with blue print

39–40   Plaid with crosses in the center (two colorways)

41–45   Floral stripe (five colorways)

46–47   Leaf print on blue or aqua ground (two colorways)

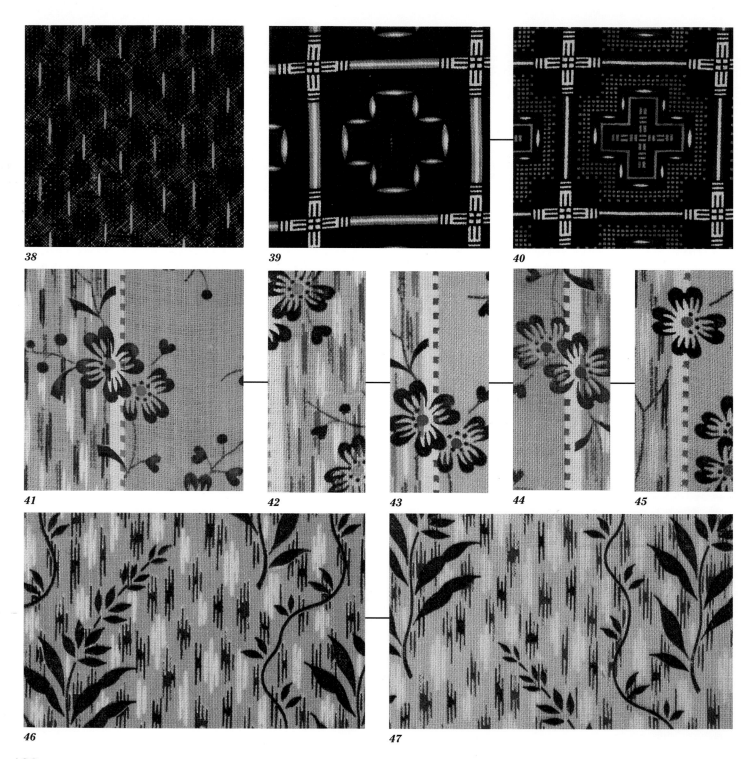

38   *39*   *40*

41   *42*   *43*   *44*   *45*

46   *47*

1902

48–51   Large dot print (four colorways)
   52   Leaf print
   53   Floral print
54–55   Brown crosses on brown ground (two colorways)

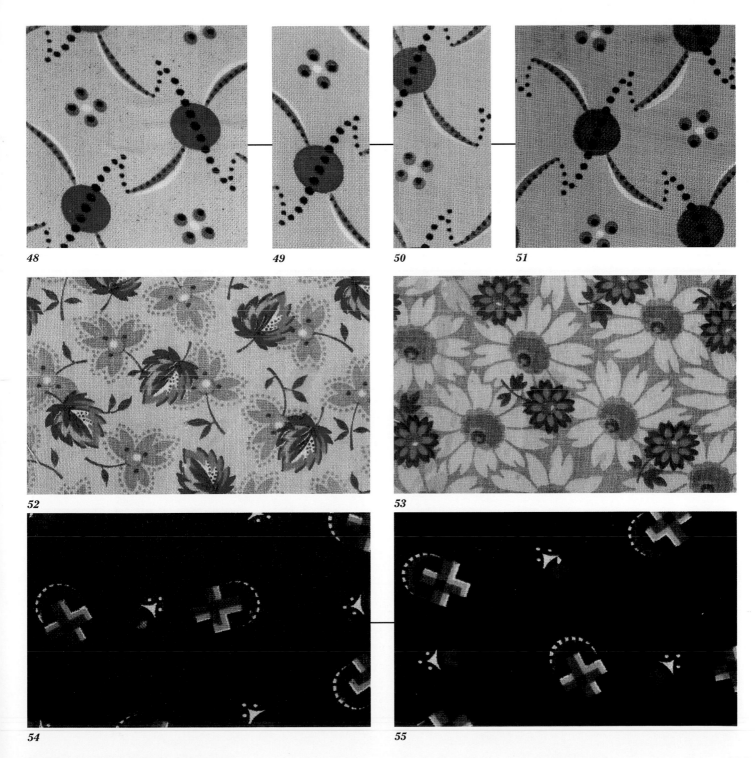

48   49   50   51

52   53

54   55

1902

56   Chained stripe

57–58   Leaf and tulip print (two colorways)

59   Blue print on brown

60   Leaf and floral print

61–62   Teal and gold floral print (two colorways)

63–64   Leaves and berries (two colorways)

65   Large white flowers on claret ground

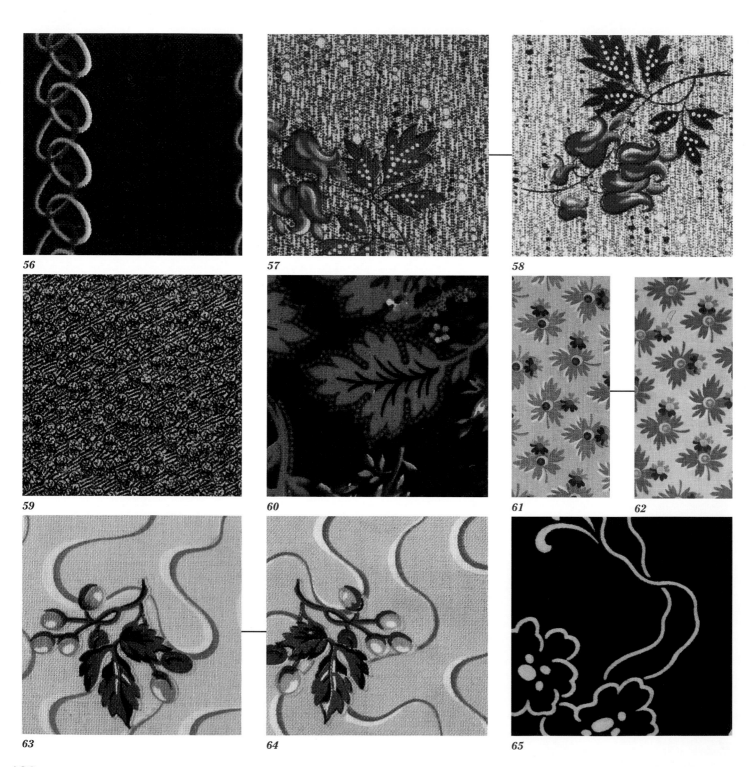

56

57

58

59

60

61

62

63

64

65

1902

66–67 Pink or lavender on white ground (two colorways)

68 Floral print on tan ground

69 Branch with leaves and teal sprigs on light teal ground

70–71 Leaves and flowers in purple or green (two colorways)

72 Blue circles on tan diagonal-stripe ground

73–74 Crescents on light ground (two colorways)

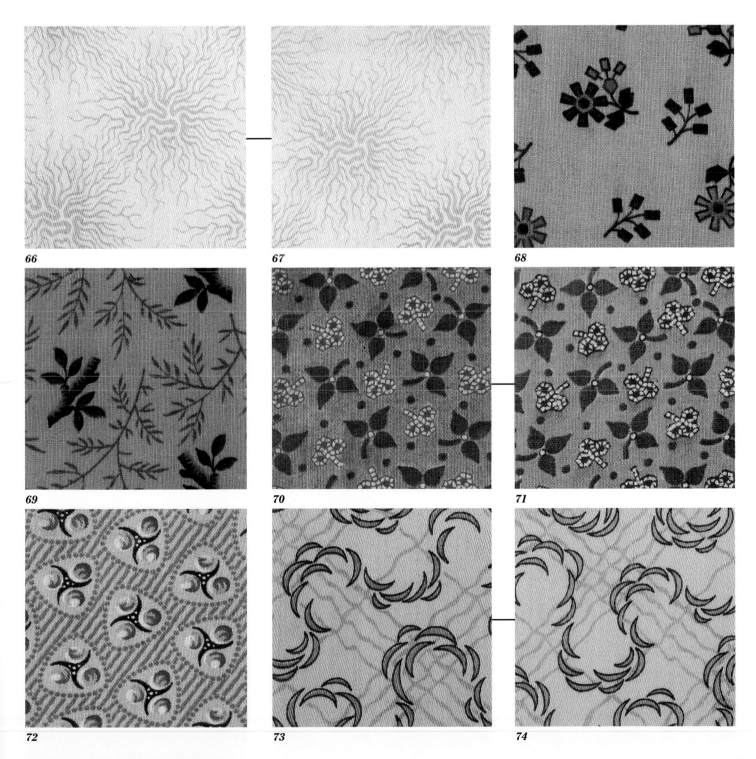

66

67

68

69

70

71

72

73

74

POOR BROTHERS' SALESMAN SAMPLES

1902

- 75   Brown and red plaid
- 76   Pink hearts with flowers
- 77–78   Lavender on teal or brown on gray ground (two colorways)
- 79–82   Geometric leaf print (four colorways)

75

76

77

78

79

80

81

82

1902

83 Purple on lavender print

84 Brown on rust print

85 Triangles and flowers

86–89 Paisley shapes (four colorways)

90 Peach-colored flowers on blue ground

91–92 Flowers on tan or aqua ground (two colorways)

83

84

85

86

87

88

89

90

91

92

1902

93   Peach flowers on pink ground

94   Lavender and teal flowers on tan ground

95–97   Flowers on blue, light green, or gray ground (three colorways)

98   Polka dots on tan ground

99   Brown flowers on tan ground

93

94

95

96

97

98

99

When we think of ticking, we are reminded of pillow ticking, which is a sturdy and thick striped cloth. Manny Kopp used this term to apply to what we commonly call shirtings, which are in the neats category.

01 Blue and black on cream, 1850–1875

02 Red and black stripe on white ticking, 1900–1925

03 Blue and red print, 1850–1875

04 Blue alphabet print, 1875–1900

05 Blue-printed check/plaid, 1875–1900

06 Red and black stripe, ca. 1900

07–08 Black-stripe dimity-weave shirtings, ca. 1900 (two colorways)

09–10 Ticking stripes, 1900–1925

11–13 Striped dimity-weave shirtings, ca. 1900

14–16 Dimity-weave neats, ca. 1900

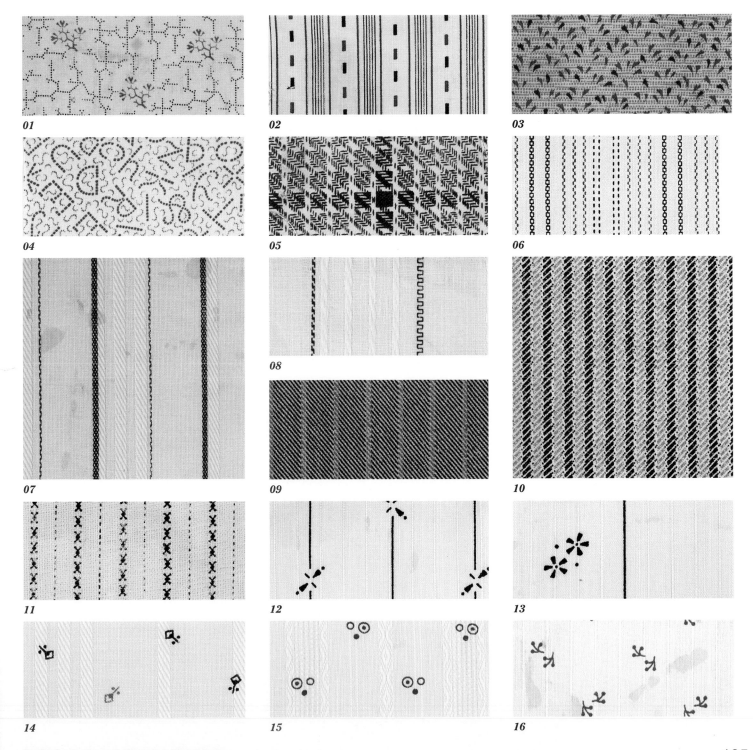

01

02

03

04

05

06

07

08

09

10

11

12

13

14

15

16

SHIRTINGS AND TICKINGS

17–19 Dimity-weave striped shirtings, ca. 1900

20 Blue-and-white check, ca. 1900

21 Red with blue-striped ticking, ca. 1900

22 Red-stripe dimity-weave shirting, ca. 1900

23 Blue-stripe dimity-weave shirting, ca. 1900

24 Blue-stripe dimity-weave shirting, ca. 1900

25–32 Ticking stripes, 1900–1925

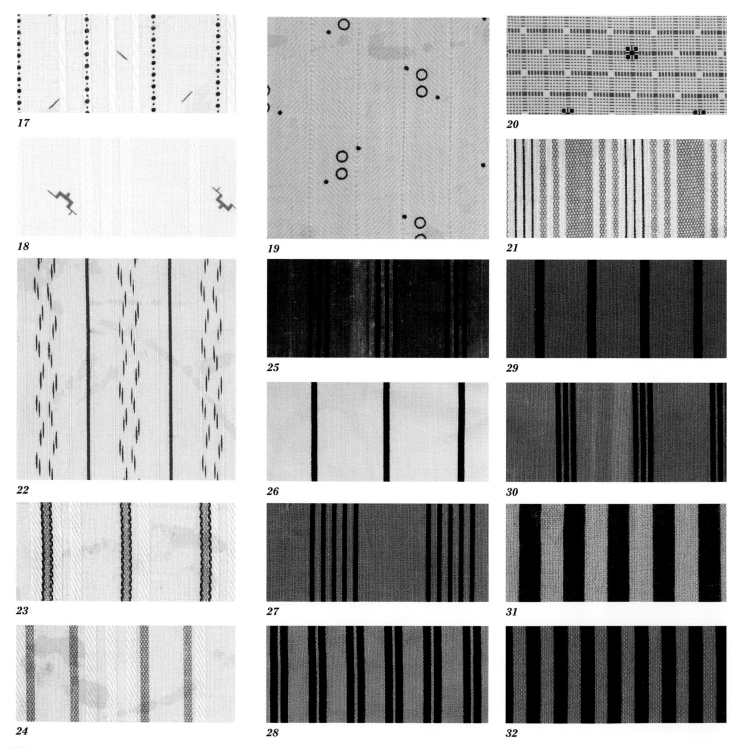

17

18

19

20

21

22

23

24

25

26

27

28

29

30

31

32

Historically, silk was a symbol of wealth and luxury and remains popular today with clothing designers as well as interior decorators. Silk accepts dye well and remains soft and supple after the dyeing process. China's economy depended on the silk industry for trade to the Romans and many other civilizations until the 1400s, when monks smuggled the secret of production out of China.

Silk was imported to America via England from 1720 to 1820 and was used for both dress and home furnishings. America had a silkworm industry in the south, but the raw product was shipped to England to be made into cloth. The industry struggled during the latter part of the eighteenth century. Several attempts to revive silkworm production in America occurred, including efforts by Brigham Young to introduce this industry to the Mormon community. In the end, he was not successful.

01 White circles on blue ground, ca. 1900

02 Pink figures on black, ca. 1900

03–04 Tan or blue flowers on black ground, ca. 1900 (two colorways)

05–07 Floral print on dark ground, ca. 1900 (three colorways)

08–09 Silk brocade paisley, 1875–1900

10–11 Pink flowers on black ground, ca. 1900 (two colorways)

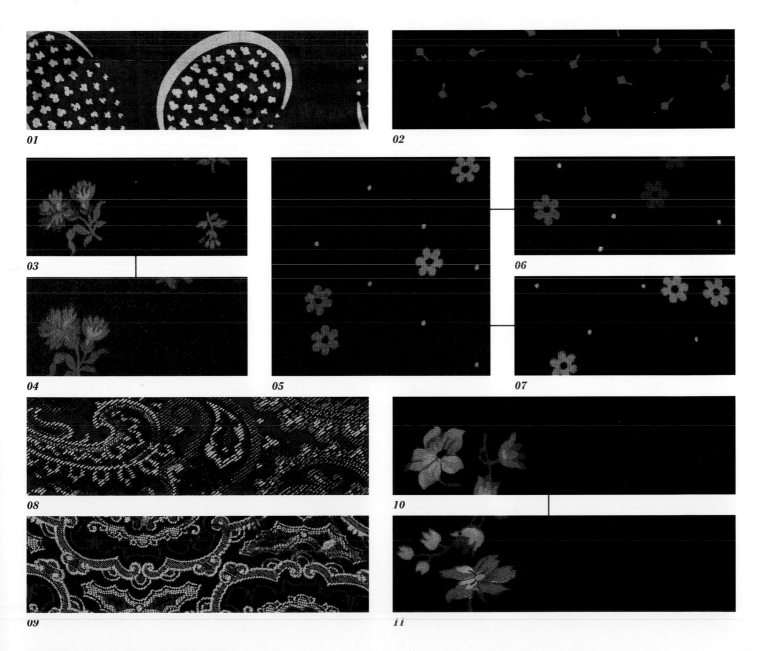

01

02

03

04

05

06

07

08

09

10

11

SILKS

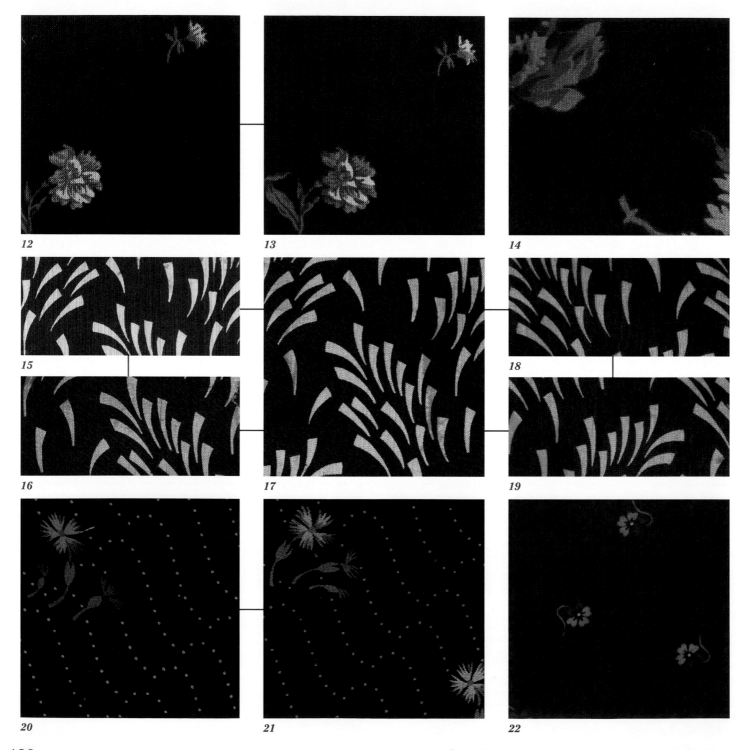

12

13

14

15

16

17

18

19

20

21

22

23–25 Flowers on dark grounds, ca. 1900 (three colorways)

26–27 Geometric design on dark grounds, ca. 1900 (two colorways)

28–29 Geometric design on dark grounds, ca. 1900 (two colorways)

30–32 Geometric design on dark grounds, ca. 1900 (three colorways)

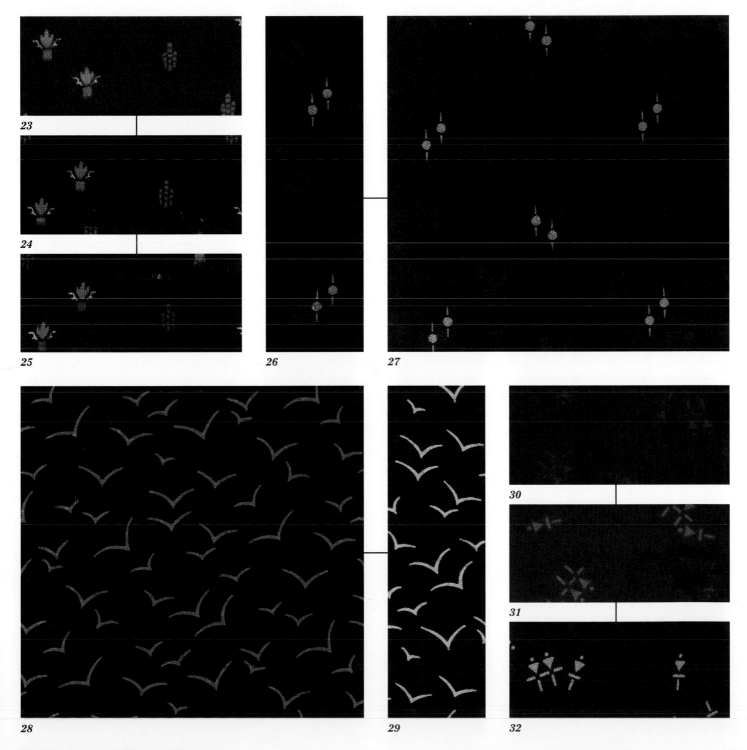

23

24

25

26

27

28

29

30

31

32

GLOSSARY

Art nouveau

According to the *World Book Encyclopedia*, art nouveau was a decorative style of design that flourished from the 1890s until about 1910. The term art nouveau means "new art" in French. It comes from the name of a Paris gallery, Maison de l'Art Nouveau, which exhibited works created in this style. Art nouveau style was ornate and was characterized by long, flowing lines that twisted in snakelike fashion. It was mainly used for interior decoration and in the design of glassware, jewelry, and other ornamental objects.

Ashton, William

William Adolphus Ashton was born in England in 1803, and immigrated to America in 1834 with his brother, John Whiteley Ashton. According to Manny's notes, William was a premier English textile designer, and he and his brother were among the first to introduce calicos to America. During this period of the mid-to-late 1830s, French calico designs were all the rage in America, but were very expensive to import. William Ashton is credited with copying the French designs for American production, thus making them affordable to purchase. It appears that copying the designs of others was commonplace at this time in history with England, France, and America partaking of this practice. Many samples of Ashton's designs are included in Manny's collection of fabric swatches. Ashton went on to design patterns for oilcloth, but eventually left the textile business and became a doctor, practicing medicine in Indiana.

Bandana prints

Bandana originated from the Hindi word *bandhnu*, which is a method of tie-dyeing. Originally oversized men's handkerchiefs, these prints are associated with the need for cowboys to protect their necks from the sun and the elements. Later, function was not as important as design and subject matter. These bordered cloths eventually became the frame for all sorts of artistic expression, flourishing from the 1880s to the 1920s, and most popular in red or blue combined with white and/or black. Our interest lies in the style of prints that evolved from these easily identified handkerchief designs.

Bengaline

With Manny's frequent trips to France, it's no wonder that he was interested in bengaline. Earlier samples originated in India and were exported to France where the silk-corded cloth was popular with women's wear designers. This worsted cord technique was also found in wool and rayon.

Chinoiserie

(pronounced sheen waz ree with the accent on the third syllable)

Chinoiserie is a French word referring to Chinese motifs in printed textiles. The French court painter Jean Baptiste Pillement included Chinese ornamentation in his engraved plate designs in the mid-1700s. Both he and Madame de Pompadour are credited with the popularity of this romantic Western decorator style, which began in the eighteenth century and continued through two more centuries. Manny made reference to fabric designs attributed to the Jean Pillement style.

Dimity

A pattern of heavier threads woven over the surface of a finer cloth.

Garibaldi prints

The Garibaldi men were popular war heroes of Italians the world over. Giuseppe Garibaldi (1807–1882) was elected to the Italian parliament in 1874. His son, Ricciotti Garibaldi (1847–1924), was an Italian patriot who fought alongside his father against the Turks. His son (Giuseppe's grandson), Giuseppe or Peppino (1879–1950), was an Italian general who commanded Greek troops in the Balkan wars, commanded Italian volunteers in the World War I, and fought for Britain in the Boer War. He immigrated to the United States in 1924. It is said that the followers of the Garibaldi men wore red shirts. This is perhaps why Sears referred to its red and black prints as Garibaldi cloth. Robe prints or black-on-red prints were popular as large- and small-scale prints in the fourth quarter of the nineteenth century through the first quarter of the twentieth century.

Geometrics

Besides the standard geometric shapes of square, rectangle, triangle, circle, etc., other shapes included in this group are primarily non-representational. Examples include plaids, neats, cartouches, pinwheels, foulards, checks, hound's tooth, eccentrics, etc. Their design is basically linear, and various parts of a geometric pattern have a relationship in dimension and scale in a repetitious pattern.

Ground

In the printing industry, "ground" means "background."

Neats

Small-scale, evenly spaced geometric figures or floral motifs typically printed in black, blue, or red on a white ground. If the ground was a color such as purple, black, brown, red, or blue, the motifs would be white. These prints were simple to produce and therefore, inexpensive, which attributed to their popularity with both males and females of all ages.

Paisley

The original cashmere shawls from which the paisley pattern derived were woven and very expensive to purchase in England because they had to be imported. The paisley motif got its name from the town of Paisley, in Scotland, where the mechanical weaving of this style of shawl on jacquard looms increased production. Prior to this time, they had always been woven in India and by hand. Designs evolved as the need grew to appease the European market with new pattern styles. Many agree that the pear or teardrop shape found in the woven textiles of the seventeenth- and eighteenth-century cashmere shawls of India originally was intended to resemble specific parts of a fantasy plant – everything from the stem to the root. Some designs were embroidered on top of the woven goods rather than created by the actual weaving process. By 1850, the paisley designs were most often printed rather than woven, and preprinted shawl fabrics were very inexpensive. The manufacturing technique met the demand for this popular style.

Pillement, Jean Baptist

Jean Baptist Pillement was a French painter and muralist, much favored by Marie Antoinette. He often combined French landscapes with oriental figures in fanciful scenes. He painted murals in Marie Antoinette's palaces in this chinoiserie style, which eventually became so popular that silk weavers in the late eighteenth century imitated many of his compositions. The popularity of Pillement's designs soon carried over into the cloth-printing industry and is still in demand today.

Steel mill engravings

These are the fine-detailed designs created by master engravers on steel rollers. The earlier the roller, the smaller the diameter, therefore, the smaller the repeat. Dyes were derived from vegetables, berries, and plants, including tree bark, as well as earth pigments. Many additives and processes were used to make the dyes fast and colorfast.

Tickings

Usually referred to as shirtings today, these are prints with small designs printed in one or two colors on a white background.

BIBLIOGRAPHY

Affleck, Diane L. Fagan. *Just New from the Mills.* Lowell, MA: American Textile History Museum, 1987.

The American College Dictionary. New York: Random House, Inc., 1964.

Berenson, Kathryn. *Quilts of Provence, The Art and Craft of French Quiltmaking.* New York: Henry Holt and Company, Inc., 1996.

Brackman, Barbara. *Clues in the Calico.* McLean, VA: EPM Publications, Inc., 1989.

Bredif, Josette. *Printed French Fabrics, Toiles de Jouy.* New York: Rizzoli, 1989.

The Columbia Encyclopedia, Third Edition, New York: Columbia University Press, 1968.

Flemming, Ernst and Renate Jaques. *Encyclopedia of Textiles.* New York: Frederick A. Praeger, 1959.

Guy, John. *Woven Cargoes, Indian Textiles in the East.* New York: Thames and Hudson, 1998.

Harris, Jennifer, ed. *Textiles: 5,000 Years.* New York: Harry N. Abrams, Inc., 1993.

Hochberg, Bette. *Spin Span Spun, Fact and Folklore for Spinners and Weavers.* Santa Cruz, CA: Bette Hochberg, publisher, 1979.

Meller, Susan and Joost Elffers. *Textile Designs.* New York: Harry N. Abrams, Inc., 1991.

Mendes, Valerie. *The Victoria & Albert Museum's Textile Collection: British Textiles From 1900 to 1937.* New York: Abbeville Press, Inc., Canopy Books, 1992.

Montgomery, Florence M. *Textiles in America 1650–1870.* New York: W.W. Norton, 1984.

Pettit, Florence H. *America's Printed & Painted Fabrics, 1600–1900.* New York: Hastings House, 1970.

Rothstein, Natalie, ed. *A Lady of Fashion, Barbara Johnson's Album of Styles and Fabrics.* New York: Thames and Hudson, 1987.

Sandberg, Gösta. *Indigo Textiles: Technique and History.* Asheville, NC: Lark Books, 1989.

Schoeser, Mary and Celia Rufey. *English and American Textiles from 1790 to the Present.* New York: Thames and Hudson, 1989.

Schoeser, Mary and Kathleen Dejardin. *French Textiles from 1760 to the Present.* London: Laurence King Ltd., 1991.

Slavin, Richard E. III. *Opulent Textiles, The Schumacher Collection.* New York: Crown Publishers, Inc., 1992.

Trestain, Eileen Jahnke. *Dating Fabrics: A Color Guide 1800–1960.* Paducah, KY: American Quilter's Society, 1998.

ABOUT THE AUTHORS

Bobbie A. Aug is a quiltmaker and collector of antique quilts and other textiles, as well as antique fabrics. She has co-authored books with Gerald E. Roy, including *Antique Quilts & Textiles: A Price Guide to Functional and Fashionable Cloth Comforts* (Collector Books, 2004), *Vintage Quilts: Identifying, Collecting, Dating, Preserving & Valuing* (Collector Books, 20042), and five books on quiltmaking with Sharon Newman. Bobbie is co-administrator of the American Quilter's Society Appraiser Certification Committee, testing and certifying appraisers of quilted textiles. She is a workshop teacher, lecturer, judge, appraiser, and a nationally recognized quilt and textile historian and resides in Colorado Springs, Colorado.

Sharon Newman was a recognized authority on nineteenth- and twentieth-century quilt patterns. Her personal quilt collection spanned two centuries of quiltmaking. Sharon enjoyed making quilts that replicated antique quilts, taught workshops, and authored several books on quiltmaking. She resided in Lubbock, Texas, and was a quilt historian and quilt appraiser certified by The American Quilter's Society. Sharon passed away in June 2005. She will be missed.

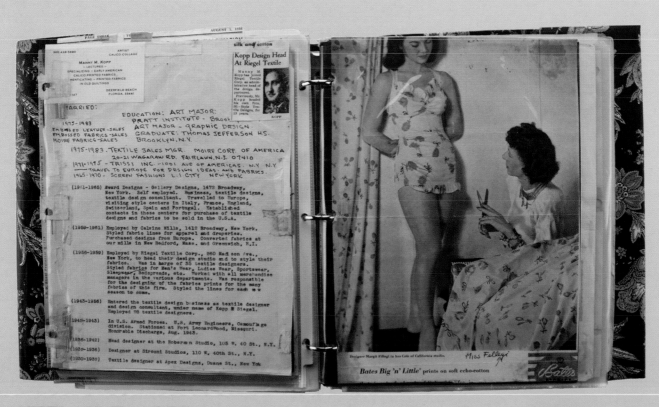

OTHER AQS BOOKS

This is only a small selection of the books available from the American Quilter's Society. AQS books are known worldwide for timely topics, clear writing, beautiful color photos, and accurate illustrations and patterns. The following books are available from your local bookseller, quilt shop, or public library.

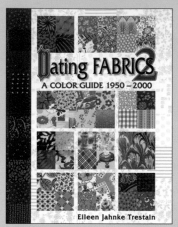

#6796 (HB) 6" x 9"   us$25.95

#6036 (HB)   us$24.95

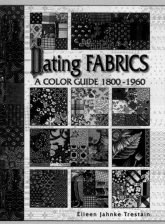

#4827 (HB) 6" x 9"   us$24.95

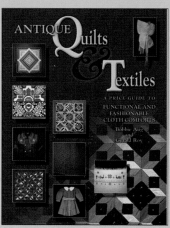

#6447 (HB)   us$24.95

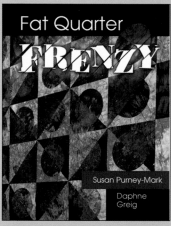

#6673   us$21.95

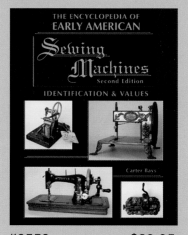

#6558 (HB)   us$29.95

#6841   us$19.95

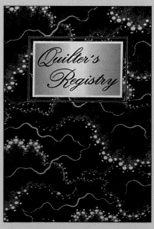

#2380 5½" x 8½"   us$9.95

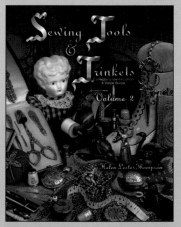

#6038 (HB)   us$24.95

Look for these books nationally.
Call or Visit our Web site at

1-800-626-5420
www.AmericanQuilter.com